C-1930 CAREER EXAMINATION SERIES

This is your PASSBOOK for...

Senior Library Clerk

Test Preparation Study Guide Questions & Answers

NLC®

NATIONAL LEARNING CORPORATION®

COPYRIGHT NOTICE

National Learning Corporation

212 Michael Drive, Syosset, NY 11791
(516) 921-8888 • www.passbooks.com
E-mail: info@passbooks.com

PUBLISHED IN THE UNITED STATES OF AMERICA

PASSBOOK® SERIES

THE *PASSBOOK® SERIES* has been created to prepare applicants and candidates for the ultimate academic battlefield – the examination room.

At some time in our lives, each and every one of us may be required to take an examination – for validation, matriculation, admission, qualification, registration, certification, or licensure.

Based on the assumption that every applicant or candidate has met the basic formal educational standards, has taken the required number of courses, and read the necessary texts, the *PASSBOOK® SERIES* furnishes the one special preparation which may assure passing with confidence, instead of failing with insecurity. Examination questions – together with answers – are furnished as the basic vehicle for study so that the mysteries of the examination and its compounding difficulties may be eliminated or diminished by a sure method.

This book is meant to help you pass your examination provided that you qualify and are serious in your objective.

The entire field is reviewed through the huge store of content information which is succinctly presented through a provocative and challenging approach – the question-and-answer method.

A climate of success is established by furnishing the correct answers at the end of each test.

You soon learn to recognize types of questions, forms of questions, and patterns of questioning. You may even begin to anticipate expected outcomes.

You perceive that many questions are repeated or adapted so that you can gain acute insights, which may enable you to score many sure points.

You learn how to confront new questions, or types of questions, and to attack them confidently and work out the correct answers.

You note objectives and emphases, and recognize pitfalls and dangers, so that you may make positive educational adjustments.

Moreover, you are kept fully informed in relation to new concepts, methods, practices, and directions in the field.

You discover that you are actually taking the examination all the time: you are preparing for the examination by "taking" an examination, not by reading extraneous and/or supererogatory textbooks.

In short, this PASSBOOK®, used directedly, should be an important factor in helping you to pass your test.

SENIOR LIBRARY CLERK

DUTIES:

Performs varied and complex library clerical duties which require prior training and knowledge of library practices and the operation of a computerized library management system.

Under general supervision of a Principal Library Clerk, Librarian, or Library Media Specialist, incumbents of this class supervise and/or perform moderately complex library clerical tasks in a functional unit of a library, i.e., circulation, technical services, etc. The incumbent receives general instructions from a Principal Library Clerk or professional position and then plans, assigns and reviews the work of a small number of clerical workers. In the absence of supervisory responsibilities, the Senior Library Clerk performs more difficult clerical work requiring a higher degree of skill, experience and independent judgment. Unusual or difficult procedures or questions are referred to the Librarian or Library Media Specialist in charge of the functional unit for decision. A Senior Library Clerk may be required to assist in the training of new clerical employees. Supervision may be exercised over Library Clerks, Pages and volunteers.

This position involves moderately complex library clerical work entailing a wide variety of data processing and clerical tasks that require previous library training or knowledge of library techniques, computer skills, and customer service skills. This class is distinguished from Library Clerks by the complexity of tasks, the responsibility for acting as a lead worker, and the exercise of independent judgment in selecting the best of a number of prescribed alternatives regarding clerical operations or interpretation of library policies. The work is performed under the direct supervision of a professional Librarian or other supervisory personnel. Incumbents may direct, review and supervise the work of subordinate clerical staff including, but not limited to, Library Clerks. Does related work as required.

SUBJECT OF EXAMINATION:

The written test is designed to evaluate knowledge, skills and/or abilities in the following areas:

1. **Fundamentals of Working in a Library** - These questions are designed to evaluate the candidate's knowledge about the common terms and concepts used in various sections of a library (e.g. circulation, reference, technical processing, etc.); the procedures associated with shelving, storing, checking out and receiving library materials; and the proper methods of using equipment commonly found in a library and of handling, processing and storing library materials.
2. **Name and Number Checking** - These questions test for the ability to distinguish between sets of words, letters, and/or numbers that are almost exactly alike. Material is usually presented in two or three columns, and you will have to determine how the entry in the first column compares with the entry in the second column and possibly the third. You will be instructed to mark your answers according to a designated code provided in the directions.
3. **Office Record Keeping** - These questions test your ability to perform common office record keeping tasks. The test consists of two or more "sets" of questions, each set concerning a different problem. Typical record keeping problems might involve the organization or collation of data from several sources; scheduling; maintaining a record system using running balances; or completion of a table summarizing data using totals, subtotals, averages and percents.

HOW TO TAKE A TEST

I. YOU MUST PASS AN EXAMINATION

A. WHAT EVERY CANDIDATE SHOULD KNOW

Examination applicants often ask us for help in preparing for the written test. What can I study in advance? What kinds of questions will be asked? How will the test be given? How will the papers be graded?

As an applicant for a civil service examination, you may be wondering about some of these things. Our purpose here is to suggest effective methods of advance study and to describe civil service examinations.

Your chances for success on this examination can be increased if you know how to prepare. Those "pre-examination jitters" can be reduced if you know what to expect. You can even experience an adventure in good citizenship if you know why civil service exams are given.

B. WHY ARE CIVIL SERVICE EXAMINATIONS GIVEN?

Civil service examinations are important to you in two ways. As a citizen, you want public jobs filled by employees who know how to do their work. As a job seeker, you want a fair chance to compete for that job on an equal footing with other candidates. The best-known means of accomplishing this two-fold goal is the competitive examination.

Exams are widely publicized throughout the nation. They may be administered for jobs in federal, state, city, municipal, town or village governments or agencies.

Any citizen may apply, with some limitations, such as the age or residence of applicants. Your experience and education may be reviewed to see whether you meet the requirements for the particular examination. When these requirements exist, they are reasonable and applied consistently to all applicants. Thus, a competitive examination may cause you some uneasiness now, but it is your privilege and safeguard.

C. HOW ARE CIVIL SERVICE EXAMS DEVELOPED?

Examinations are carefully written by trained technicians who are specialists in the field known as "psychological measurement," in consultation with recognized authorities in the field of work that the test will cover. These experts recommend the subject matter areas or skills to be tested; only those knowledges or skills important to your success on the job are included. The most reliable books and source materials available are used as references. Together, the experts and technicians judge the difficulty level of the questions.

Test technicians know how to phrase questions so that the problem is clearly stated. Their ethics do not permit "trick" or "catch" questions. Questions may have been tried out on sample groups, or subjected to statistical analysis, to determine their usefulness.

Written tests are often used in combination with performance tests, ratings of training and experience, and oral interviews. All of these measures combine to form the best-known means of finding the right person for the right job.

II. HOW TO PASS THE WRITTEN TEST

A. NATURE OF THE EXAMINATION

To prepare intelligently for civil service examinations, you should know how they differ from school examinations you have taken. In school you were assigned certain definite pages to read or subjects to cover. The examination questions were quite detailed and usually emphasized memory. Civil service exams, on the other hand, try to discover your present ability to perform the duties of a position, plus your potentiality to learn these duties. In other words, a civil service exam attempts to predict how successful you will be. Questions cover such a broad area that they cannot be as minute and detailed as school exam questions.

In the public service similar kinds of work, or positions, are grouped together in one "class." This process is known as *position-classification*. All the positions in a class are paid according to the salary range for that class. One class title covers all of these positions, and they are all tested by the same examination.

B. FOUR BASIC STEPS

1) Study the announcement

How, then, can you know what subjects to study? Our best answer is: "Learn as much as possible about the class of positions for which you've applied." The exam will test the knowledge, skills and abilities needed to do the work.

Your most valuable source of information about the position you want is the official exam announcement. This announcement lists the training and experience qualifications. Check these standards and apply only if you come reasonably close to meeting them.

The brief description of the position in the examination announcement offers some clues to the subjects which will be tested. Think about the job itself. Review the duties in your mind. Can you perform them, or are there some in which you are rusty? Fill in the blank spots in your preparation.

Many jurisdictions preview the written test in the exam announcement by including a section called "Knowledge and Abilities Required," "Scope of the Examination," or some similar heading. Here you will find out specifically what fields will be tested.

2) Review your own background

Once you learn in general what the position is all about, and what you need to know to do the work, ask yourself which subjects you already know fairly well and which need improvement. You may wonder whether to concentrate on improving your strong areas or on building some background in your fields of weakness. When the announcement has specified "some knowledge" or "considerable knowledge," or has used adjectives like "beginning principles of…" or "advanced … methods," you can get a clue as to the number and difficulty of questions to be asked in any given field. More questions, and hence broader coverage, would be included for those subjects which are more important in the work. Now weigh your strengths and weaknesses against the job requirements and prepare accordingly.

3) Determine the level of the position

Another way to tell how intensively you should prepare is to understand the level of the job for which you are applying. Is it the entering level? In other words, is this the position in which beginners in a field of work are hired? Or is it an intermediate or advanced level? Sometimes this is indicated by such words as "Junior" or "Senior" in the class title. Other jurisdictions use Roman numerals to designate the level – Clerk I, Clerk II, for example. The word "Supervisor" sometimes appears in the title. If the level is not indicated by the title, check the description of duties. Will you be working under very close supervision, or will you have responsibility for independent decisions in this work?

4) Choose appropriate study materials

Now that you know the subjects to be examined and the relative amount of each subject to be covered, you can choose suitable study materials. For beginning level jobs, or even advanced ones, if you have a pronounced weakness in some aspect of your training, read a modern, standard textbook in that field. Be sure it is up to date and has general coverage. Such books are normally available at your library, and the librarian will be glad to help you locate one. For entry-level positions, questions of appropriate difficulty are chosen – neither highly advanced questions, nor those too simple. Such questions require careful thought but not advanced training.

If the position for which you are applying is technical or advanced, you will read more advanced, specialized material. If you are already familiar with the basic principles of your field, elementary textbooks would waste your time. Concentrate on advanced textbooks and technical periodicals. Think through the concepts and review difficult problems in your field.

These are all general sources. You can get more ideas on your own initiative, following these leads. For example, training manuals and publications of the government agency which employs workers in your field can be useful, particularly for technical and professional positions. A letter or visit to the government department involved may result in more specific study suggestions, and certainly will provide you with a more definite idea of the exact nature of the position you are seeking.

III. KINDS OF TESTS

Tests are used for purposes other than measuring knowledge and ability to perform specified duties. For some positions, it is equally important to test ability to make adjustments to new situations or to profit from training. In others, basic mental abilities not dependent on information are essential. Questions which test these things may not appear as pertinent to the duties of the position as those which test for knowledge and information. Yet they are often highly important parts of a fair examination. For very general questions, it is almost impossible to help you direct your study efforts. What we can do is to point out some of the more common of these general abilities needed in public service positions and describe some typical questions.

1) General information

Broad, general information has been found useful for predicting job success in some kinds of work. This is tested in a variety of ways, from vocabulary lists to questions about current events. Basic background in some field of work, such as sociology or economics, may be sampled in a group of questions. Often these are principles which have become familiar to most persons through exposure rather than through formal training. It is difficult to advise you how to study for these questions; being alert to the world around you is our best suggestion.

2) Verbal ability

An example of an ability needed in many positions is verbal or language ability. Verbal ability is, in brief, the ability to use and understand words. Vocabulary and grammar tests are typical measures of this ability. Reading comprehension or paragraph interpretation questions are common in many kinds of civil service tests. You are given a paragraph of written material and asked to find its central meaning.

3) Numerical ability

Number skills can be tested by the familiar arithmetic problem, by checking paired lists of numbers to see which are alike and which are different, or by interpreting charts and graphs. In the latter test, a graph may be printed in the test booklet which you are asked to use as the basis for answering questions.

4) Observation

A popular test for law-enforcement positions is the observation test. A picture is shown to you for several minutes, then taken away. Questions about the picture test your ability to observe both details and larger elements.

5) Following directions

In many positions in the public service, the employee must be able to carry out written instructions dependably and accurately. You may be given a chart with several columns, each column listing a variety of information. The questions require you to carry out directions involving the information given in the chart.

6) Skills and aptitudes

Performance tests effectively measure some manual skills and aptitudes. When the skill is one in which you are trained, such as typing or shorthand, you can practice. These tests are often very much like those given in business school or high school courses. For many of the other skills and aptitudes, however, no short-time preparation can be made. Skills and abilities natural to you or that you have developed throughout your lifetime are being tested.

Many of the general questions just described provide all the data needed to answer the questions and ask you to use your reasoning ability to find the answers. Your best preparation for these tests, as well as for tests of facts and ideas, is to be at your physical and mental best. You, no doubt, have your own methods of getting into an exam-taking mood and keeping "in shape." The next section lists some ideas on this subject.

IV. KINDS OF QUESTIONS

Only rarely is the "essay" question, which you answer in narrative form, used in civil service tests. Civil service tests are usually of the short-answer type. Full instructions for answering these questions will be given to you at the examination. But in case this is your first experience with short-answer questions and separate answer sheets, here is what you need to know:

1) Multiple-choice Questions

Most popular of the short-answer questions is the "multiple choice" or "best answer" question. It can be used, for example, to test for factual knowledge, ability to solve problems or judgment in meeting situations found at work.

A multiple-choice question is normally one of three types—

- It can begin with an incomplete statement followed by several possible endings. You are to find the one ending which *best* completes the statement, although some of the others may not be entirely wrong.
- It can also be a complete statement in the form of a question which is answered by choosing one of the statements listed.

- It can be in the form of a problem – again you select the best answer.

Here is an example of a multiple-choice question with a discussion which should give you some clues as to the method for choosing the right answer:

When an employee has a complaint about his assignment, the action which will *best* help him overcome his difficulty is to

A. discuss his difficulty with his coworkers
B. take the problem to the head of the organization
C. take the problem to the person who gave him the assignment
D. say nothing to anyone about his complaint

In answering this question, you should study each of the choices to find which is best. Consider choice "A" – Certainly an employee may discuss his complaint with fellow employees, but no change or improvement can result, and the complaint remains unresolved. Choice "B" is a poor choice since the head of the organization probably does not know what assignment you have been given, and taking your problem to him is known as "going over the head" of the supervisor. The supervisor, or person who made the assignment, is the person who can clarify it or correct any injustice. Choice "C" is, therefore, correct. To say nothing, as in choice "D," is unwise. Supervisors have and interest in knowing the problems employees are facing, and the employee is seeking a solution to his problem.

2) True/False Questions

The "true/false" or "right/wrong" form of question is sometimes used. Here a complete statement is given. Your job is to decide whether the statement is right or wrong.

SAMPLE: A roaming cell-phone call to a nearby city costs less than a non-roaming call to a distant city.

This statement is wrong, or false, since roaming calls are more expensive.

This is not a complete list of all possible question forms, although most of the others are variations of these common types. You will always get complete directions for answering questions. Be sure you understand *how* to mark your answers – ask questions until you do.

V. RECORDING YOUR ANSWERS

Computer terminals are used more and more today for many different kinds of exams.

For an examination with very few applicants, you may be told to record your answers in the test booklet itself. Separate answer sheets are much more common. If this separate answer sheet is to be scored by machine – and this is often the case – it is highly important that you mark your answers correctly in order to get credit.

An electronic scoring machine is often used in civil service offices because of the speed with which papers can be scored. Machine-scored answer sheets must be marked with a pencil, which will be given to you. This pencil has a high graphite content which responds to the electronic scoring machine. As a matter of fact, stray dots may register as answers, so do not let your pencil rest on the answer sheet while you are pondering the correct answer. Also, if your pencil lead breaks or is otherwise defective, ask for another.

Since the answer sheet will be dropped in a slot in the scoring machine, be careful not to bend the corners or get the paper crumpled.

The answer sheet normally has five vertical columns of numbers, with 30 numbers to a column. These numbers correspond to the question numbers in your test booklet. After each number, going across the page are four or five pairs of dotted lines. These short dotted lines have small letters or numbers above them. The first two pairs may also have a "T" or "F" above the letters. This indicates that the first two pairs only are to be used if the questions are of the true-false type. If the questions are multiple choice, disregard the "T" and "F" and pay attention only to the small letters or numbers.

Answer your questions in the manner of the sample that follows:

32. The largest city in the United States is
    A. Washington, D.C.
    B. New York City
    C. Chicago
    D. Detroit
    E. San Francisco

1) Choose the answer you think is best. (New York City is the largest, so "B" is correct.)
2) Find the row of dotted lines numbered the same as the question you are answering. (Find row number 32)
3) Find the pair of dotted lines corresponding to the answer. (Find the pair of lines under the mark "B.")
4) Make a solid black mark between the dotted lines.

VI. BEFORE THE TEST

Common sense will help you find procedures to follow to get ready for an examination. Too many of us, however, overlook these sensible measures. Indeed, nervousness and fatigue have been found to be the most serious reasons why applicants fail to do their best on civil service tests. Here is a list of reminders:

- Begin your preparation early – Don't wait until the last minute to go scurrying around for books and materials or to find out what the position is all about.
- Prepare continuously – An hour a night for a week is better than an all-night cram session. This has been definitely established. What is more, a night a week for a month will return better dividends than crowding your study into a shorter period of time.
- Locate the place of the exam – You have been sent a notice telling you when and where to report for the examination. If the location is in a different town or otherwise unfamiliar to you, it would be well to inquire the best route and learn something about the building.
- Relax the night before the test – Allow your mind to rest. Do not study at all that night. Plan some mild recreation or diversion; then go to bed early and get a good night's sleep.
- Get up early enough to make a leisurely trip to the place for the test – This way unforeseen events, traffic snarls, unfamiliar buildings, etc. will not upset you.
- Dress comfortably – A written test is not a fashion show. You will be known by number and not by name, so wear something comfortable.

- Leave excess paraphernalia at home – Shopping bags and odd bundles will get in your way. You need bring only the items mentioned in the official notice you received; usually everything you need is provided. Do not bring reference books to the exam. They will only confuse those last minutes and be taken away from you when in the test room.
- Arrive somewhat ahead of time – If because of transportation schedules you must get there very early, bring a newspaper or magazine to take your mind off yourself while waiting.
- Locate the examination room – When you have found the proper room, you will be directed to the seat or part of the room where you will sit. Sometimes you are given a sheet of instructions to read while you are waiting. Do not fill out any forms until you are told to do so; just read them and be prepared.
- Relax and prepare to listen to the instructions
- If you have any physical problem that may keep you from doing your best, be sure to tell the test administrator. If you are sick or in poor health, you really cannot do your best on the exam. You can come back and take the test some other time.

VII. AT THE TEST

The day of the test is here and you have the test booklet in your hand. The temptation to get going is very strong. Caution! There is more to success than knowing the right answers. You must know how to identify your papers and understand variations in the type of short-answer question used in this particular examination. Follow these suggestions for maximum results from your efforts:

1) Cooperate with the monitor

The test administrator has a duty to create a situation in which you can be as much at ease as possible. He will give instructions, tell you when to begin, check to see that you are marking your answer sheet correctly, and so on. He is not there to guard you, although he will see that your competitors do not take unfair advantage. He wants to help you do your best.

2) Listen to all instructions

Don't jump the gun! Wait until you understand all directions. In most civil service tests you get more time than you need to answer the questions. So don't be in a hurry. Read each word of instructions until you clearly understand the meaning. Study the examples, listen to all announcements and follow directions. Ask questions if you do not understand what to do.

3) Identify your papers

Civil service exams are usually identified by number only. You will be assigned a number; you must not put your name on your test papers. Be sure to copy your number correctly. Since more than one exam may be given, copy your exact examination title.

4) Plan your time

Unless you are told that a test is a "speed" or "rate of work" test, speed itself is usually not important. Time enough to answer all the questions will be provided, but this does not mean that you have all day. An overall time limit has been set. Divide the total time (in minutes) by the number of questions to determine the approximate time you have for each question.

5) Do not linger over difficult questions

If you come across a difficult question, mark it with a paper clip (useful to have along) and come back to it when you have been through the booklet. One caution if you do this – be sure to skip a number on your answer sheet as well. Check often to be sure that you have not lost your place and that you are marking in the row numbered the same as the question you are answering.

6) Read the questions

Be sure you know what the question asks! Many capable people are unsuccessful because they failed to *read* the questions correctly.

7) Answer all questions

Unless you have been instructed that a penalty will be deducted for incorrect answers, it is better to guess than to omit a question.

8) Speed tests

It is often better NOT to guess on speed tests. It has been found that on timed tests people are tempted to spend the last few seconds before time is called in marking answers at random – without even reading them – in the hope of picking up a few extra points. To discourage this practice, the instructions may warn you that your score will be "corrected" for guessing. That is, a penalty will be applied. The incorrect answers will be deducted from the correct ones, or some other penalty formula will be used.

9) Review your answers

If you finish before time is called, go back to the questions you guessed or omitted to give them further thought. Review other answers if you have time.

10) Return your test materials

If you are ready to leave before others have finished or time is called, take ALL your materials to the monitor and leave quietly. Never take any test material with you. The monitor can discover whose papers are not complete, and taking a test booklet may be grounds for disqualification.

VIII. EXAMINATION TECHNIQUES

1) Read the general instructions carefully. These are usually printed on the first page of the exam booklet. As a rule, these instructions refer to the timing of the examination; the fact that you should not start work until the signal and must stop work at a signal, etc. If there are any *special* instructions, such as a choice of questions to be answered, make sure that you note this instruction carefully.

2) When you are ready to start work on the examination, that is as soon as the signal has been given, read the instructions to each question booklet, underline any key words or phrases, such as *least*, *best*, *outline*, *describe* and the like. In this way you will tend to answer as requested rather than discover on reviewing your paper that you *listed without describing*, that you selected the *worst* choice rather than the *best* choice, etc.

3) If the examination is of the objective or multiple-choice type – that is, each question will also give a series of possible answers: A, B, C or D, and you are called upon to select the best answer and write the letter next to that answer on your answer paper – it is advisable to start answering each question in turn. There may be anywhere from 50 to 100 such questions in the three or four hours allotted and you can see how much time would be taken if you read through all the questions before beginning to answer any. Furthermore, if you come across a question or group of questions which you know would be difficult to answer, it would undoubtedly affect your handling of all the other questions.

4) If the examination is of the essay type and contains but a few questions, it is a moot point as to whether you should read all the questions before starting to answer any one. Of course, if you are given a choice – say five out of seven and the like – then it is essential to read all the questions so you can eliminate the two that are most difficult. If, however, you are asked to answer all the questions, there may be danger in trying to answer the easiest one first because you may find that you will spend too much time on it. The best technique is to answer the first question, then proceed to the second, etc.

5) Time your answers. Before the exam begins, write down the time it started, then add the time allowed for the examination and write down the time it must be completed, then divide the time available somewhat as follows:
    - If 3-1/2 hours are allowed, that would be 210 minutes. If you have 80 objective-type questions, that would be an average of 2-1/2 minutes per question. Allow yourself no more than 2 minutes per question, or a total of 160 minutes, which will permit about 50 minutes to review.
    - If for the time allotment of 210 minutes there are 7 essay questions to answer, that would average about 30 minutes a question. Give yourself only 25 minutes per question so that you have about 35 minutes to review.

6) The most important instruction is to *read each question* and make sure you know what is wanted. The second most important instruction is to *time yourself properly* so that you answer every question. The third most important instruction is to *answer every question*. Guess if you have to but include something for each question. Remember that you will receive no credit for a blank and will probably receive some credit if you write something in answer to an essay question. If you guess a letter – say "B" for a multiple-choice question – you may have guessed right. If you leave a blank as an answer to a multiple-choice question, the examiners may respect your feelings but it will not add a point to your score. Some exams may penalize you for wrong answers, so in such cases *only*, you may not want to guess unless you have some basis for your answer.

7) Suggestions
    a. Objective-type questions
        1. Examine the question booklet for proper sequence of pages and questions
        2. Read all instructions carefully
        3. Skip any question which seems too difficult; return to it after all other questions have been answered
        4. Apportion your time properly; do not spend too much time on any single question or group of questions

5. Note and underline key words – *all, most, fewest, least, best, worst, same, opposite,* etc.
6. Pay particular attention to negatives
7. Note unusual option, e.g., unduly long, short, complex, different or similar in content to the body of the question
8. Observe the use of "hedging" words – *probably, may, most likely,* etc.
9. Make sure that your answer is put next to the same number as the question
10. Do not second-guess unless you have good reason to believe the second answer is definitely more correct
11. Cross out original answer if you decide another answer is more accurate; do not erase until you are ready to hand your paper in
12. Answer all questions; guess unless instructed otherwise
13. Leave time for review

b. Essay questions
1. Read each question carefully
2. Determine exactly what is wanted. Underline key words or phrases.
3. Decide on outline or paragraph answer
4. Include many different points and elements unless asked to develop any one or two points or elements
5. Show impartiality by giving pros and cons unless directed to select one side only
6. Make and write down any assumptions you find necessary to answer the questions
7. Watch your English, grammar, punctuation and choice of words
8. Time your answers; don't crowd material

8) Answering the essay question

Most essay questions can be answered by framing the specific response around several key words or ideas. Here are a few such key words or ideas:

M's: manpower, materials, methods, money, management
P's: purpose, program, policy, plan, procedure, practice, problems, pitfalls, personnel, public relations

a. Six basic steps in handling problems:
1. Preliminary plan and background development
2. Collect information, data and facts
3. Analyze and interpret information, data and facts
4. Analyze and develop solutions as well as make recommendations
5. Prepare report and sell recommendations
6. Install recommendations and follow up effectiveness

b. Pitfalls to avoid
1. *Taking things for granted* – A statement of the situation does not necessarily imply that each of the elements is necessarily true; for example, a complaint may be invalid and biased so that all that can be taken for granted is that a complaint has been registered

2. *Considering only one side of a situation* – Wherever possible, indicate several alternatives and then point out the reasons you selected the best one
3. *Failing to indicate follow up* – Whenever your answer indicates action on your part, make certain that you will take proper follow-up action to see how successful your recommendations, procedures or actions turn out to be
4. *Taking too long in answering any single question* – Remember to time your answers properly

IX. AFTER THE TEST

Scoring procedures differ in detail among civil service jurisdictions although the general principles are the same. Whether the papers are hand-scored or graded by machine we have described, they are nearly always graded by number. That is, the person who marks the paper knows only the number – never the name – of the applicant. Not until all the papers have been graded will they be matched with names. If other tests, such as training and experience or oral interview ratings have been given, scores will be combined. Different parts of the examination usually have different weights. For example, the written test might count 60 percent of the final grade, and a rating of training and experience 40 percent. In many jurisdictions, veterans will have a certain number of points added to their grades.

After the final grade has been determined, the names are placed in grade order and an eligible list is established. There are various methods for resolving ties between those who get the same final grade – probably the most common is to place first the name of the person whose application was received first. Job offers are made from the eligible list in the order the names appear on it. You will be notified of your grade and your rank as soon as all these computations have been made. This will be done as rapidly as possible.

People who are found to meet the requirements in the announcement are called "eligibles." Their names are put on a list of eligible candidates. An eligible's chances of getting a job depend on how high he stands on this list and how fast agencies are filling jobs from the list.

When a job is to be filled from a list of eligibles, the agency asks for the names of people on the list of eligibles for that job. When the civil service commission receives this request, it sends to the agency the names of the three people highest on this list. Or, if the job to be filled has specialized requirements, the office sends the agency the names of the top three persons who meet these requirements from the general list.

The appointing officer makes a choice from among the three people whose names were sent to him. If the selected person accepts the appointment, the names of the others are put back on the list to be considered for future openings.

That is the rule in hiring from all kinds of eligible lists, whether they are for typist, carpenter, chemist, or something else. For every vacancy, the appointing officer has his choice of any one of the top three eligibles on the list. This explains why the person whose name is on top of the list sometimes does not get an appointment when some of the persons lower on the list do. If the appointing officer chooses the second or third eligible, the No. 1 eligible does not get a job at once, but stays on the list until he is appointed or the list is terminated.

X. HOW TO PASS THE INTERVIEW TEST

The examination for which you applied requires an oral interview test. You have already taken the written test and you are now being called for the interview test – the final part of the formal examination.

You may think that it is not possible to prepare for an interview test and that there are no procedures to follow during an interview. Our purpose is to point out some things you can do in advance that will help you and some good rules to follow and pitfalls to avoid while you are being interviewed.

What is an interview supposed to test?

The written examination is designed to test the technical knowledge and competence of the candidate; the oral is designed to evaluate intangible qualities, not readily measured otherwise, and to establish a list showing the relative fitness of each candidate – as measured against his competitors – for the position sought. Scoring is not on the basis of "right" and "wrong," but on a sliding scale of values ranging from "not passable" to "outstanding." As a matter of fact, it is possible to achieve a relatively low score without a single "incorrect" answer because of evident weakness in the qualities being measured.

Occasionally, an examination may consist entirely of an oral test – either an individual or a group oral. In such cases, information is sought concerning the technical knowledges and abilities of the candidate, since there has been no written examination for this purpose. More commonly, however, an oral test is used to supplement a written examination.

Who conducts interviews?

The composition of oral boards varies among different jurisdictions. In nearly all, a representative of the personnel department serves as chairman. One of the members of the board may be a representative of the department in which the candidate would work. In some cases, "outside experts" are used, and, frequently, a businessman or some other representative of the general public is asked to serve. Labor and management or other special groups may be represented. The aim is to secure the services of experts in the appropriate field.

However the board is composed, it is a good idea (and not at all improper or unethical) to ascertain in advance of the interview who the members are and what groups they represent. When you are introduced to them, you will have some idea of their backgrounds and interests, and at least you will not stutter and stammer over their names.

What should be done before the interview?

While knowledge about the board members is useful and takes some of the surprise element out of the interview, there is other preparation which is more substantive. It *is* possible to prepare for an oral interview – in several ways:

1) Keep a copy of your application and review it carefully before the interview

This may be the only document before the oral board, and the starting point of the interview. Know what education and experience you have listed there, and the sequence and dates of all of it. Sometimes the board will ask you to review the highlights of your experience for them; you should not have to hem and haw doing it.

2) Study the class specification and the examination announcement

Usually, the oral board has one or both of these to guide them. The qualities, characteristics or knowledges required by the position sought are stated in these documents. They offer valuable clues as to the nature of the oral interview. For example, if the job involves supervisory responsibilities, the announcement will usually indicate that knowledge of modern supervisory methods and the qualifications of the candidate as a supervisor will be tested. If so, you can expect such questions, frequently in the form of a hypothetical situation which you are expected to solve. NEVER go into an oral without knowledge of the duties and responsibilities of the job you seek.

3) Think through each qualification required

Try to visualize the kind of questions you would ask if you were a board member. How well could you answer them? Try especially to appraise your own knowledge and background in each area, *measured against the job sought*, and identify any areas in which you are weak. Be critical and realistic – do not flatter yourself.

4) Do some general reading in areas in which you feel you may be weak

For example, if the job involves supervision and your past experience has NOT, some general reading in supervisory methods and practices, particularly in the field of human relations, might be useful. Do NOT study agency procedures or detailed manuals. The oral board will be testing your understanding and capacity, not your memory.

5) Get a good night's sleep and watch your general health and mental attitude

You will want a clear head at the interview. Take care of a cold or any other minor ailment, and of course, no hangovers.

What should be done on the day of the interview?

Now comes the day of the interview itself. Give yourself plenty of time to get there. Plan to arrive somewhat ahead of the scheduled time, particularly if your appointment is in the fore part of the day. If a previous candidate fails to appear, the board might be ready for you a bit early. By early afternoon an oral board is almost invariably behind schedule if there are many candidates, and you may have to wait. Take along a book or magazine to read, or your application to review, but leave any extraneous material in the waiting room when you go in for your interview. In any event, relax and compose yourself.

The matter of dress is important. The board is forming impressions about you – from your experience, your manners, your attitude, and your appearance. Give your personal appearance careful attention. Dress your best, but not your flashiest. Choose conservative, appropriate clothing, and be sure it is immaculate. This is a business interview, and your appearance should indicate that you regard it as such. Besides, being well groomed and properly dressed will help boost your confidence.

Sooner or later, someone will call your name and escort you into the interview room. *This is it.* From here on you are on your own. It is too late for any more preparation. But remember, you asked for this opportunity to prove your fitness, and you are here because your request was granted.

What happens when you go in?

The usual sequence of events will be as follows: The clerk (who is often the board stenographer) will introduce you to the chairman of the oral board, who will introduce you to the other members of the board. Acknowledge the introductions before you sit down. Do not be surprised if you find a microphone facing you or a stenotypist sitting by. Oral interviews are usually recorded in the event of an appeal or other review.

Usually the chairman of the board will open the interview by reviewing the highlights of your education and work experience from your application – primarily for the benefit of the other members of the board, as well as to get the material into the record. Do not interrupt or comment unless there is an error or significant misinterpretation; if that is the case, do not hesitate. But do not quibble about insignificant matters. Also, he will usually ask you some question about your education, experience or your present job – partly to get you to start talking and to establish the interviewing "rapport." He may start the actual questioning, or turn it over to one of the other members. Frequently, each member undertakes the questioning on a particular area, one in which he is perhaps most competent, so you can expect each member to participate in the examination. Because time is limited, you may also expect some rather abrupt switches in the direction the questioning takes, so do not be upset by it. Normally, a board member will not pursue a single line of questioning unless he discovers a particular strength or weakness.

After each member has participated, the chairman will usually ask whether any member has any further questions, then will ask you if you have anything you wish to add. Unless you are expecting this question, it may floor you. Worse, it may start you off on an extended, extemporaneous speech. The board is not usually seeking more information. The question is principally to offer you a last opportunity to present further qualifications or to indicate that you have nothing to add. So, if you feel that a significant qualification or characteristic has been overlooked, it is proper to point it out in a sentence or so. Do not compliment the board on the thoroughness of their examination – they have been sketchy, and you know it. If you wish, merely say, "No thank you, I have nothing further to add." This is a point where you can "talk yourself out" of a good impression or fail to present an important bit of information. Remember, *you close the interview yourself.*

The chairman will then say, "That is all, Mr. ______, thank you." Do not be startled; the interview is over, and quicker than you think. Thank him, gather your belongings and take your leave. Save your sigh of relief for the other side of the door.

How to put your best foot forward

Throughout this entire process, you may feel that the board individually and collectively is trying to pierce your defenses, seek out your hidden weaknesses and embarrass and confuse you. Actually, this is not true. They are obliged to make an appraisal of your qualifications for the job you are seeking, and they want to see you in your best light. Remember, they must interview all candidates and a non-cooperative candidate may become a failure in spite of their best efforts to bring out his qualifications. Here are 15 suggestions that will help you:

1) Be natural – Keep your attitude confident, not cocky

If you are not confident that you can do the job, do not expect the board to be. Do not apologize for your weaknesses, try to bring out your strong points. The board is interested in a positive, not negative, presentation. Cockiness will antagonize any board member and make him wonder if you are covering up a weakness by a false show of strength.

2) Get comfortable, but don't lounge or sprawl

Sit erectly but not stiffly. A careless posture may lead the board to conclude that you are careless in other things, or at least that you are not impressed by the importance of the occasion. Either conclusion is natural, even if incorrect. Do not fuss with your clothing, a pencil or an ashtray. Your hands may occasionally be useful to emphasize a point; do not let them become a point of distraction.

3) Do not wisecrack or make small talk

This is a serious situation, and your attitude should show that you consider it as such. Further, the time of the board is limited – they do not want to waste it, and neither should you.

4) Do not exaggerate your experience or abilities

In the first place, from information in the application or other interviews and sources, the board may know more about you than you think. Secondly, you probably will not get away with it. An experienced board is rather adept at spotting such a situation, so do not take the chance.

5) If you know a board member, do not make a point of it, yet do not hide it

Certainly you are not fooling him, and probably not the other members of the board. Do not try to take advantage of your acquaintanceship – it will probably do you little good.

6) Do not dominate the interview

Let the board do that. They will give you the clues – do not assume that you have to do all the talking. Realize that the board has a number of questions to ask you, and do not try to take up all the interview time by showing off your extensive knowledge of the answer to the first one.

7) Be attentive

You only have 20 minutes or so, and you should keep your attention at its sharpest throughout. When a member is addressing a problem or question to you, give him your undivided attention. Address your reply principally to him, but do not exclude the other board members.

8) Do not interrupt

A board member may be stating a problem for you to analyze. He will ask you a question when the time comes. Let him state the problem, and wait for the question.

9) Make sure you understand the question

Do not try to answer until you are sure what the question is. If it is not clear, restate it in your own words or ask the board member to clarify it for you. However, do not haggle about minor elements.

10) Reply promptly but not hastily

A common entry on oral board rating sheets is "candidate responded readily," or "candidate hesitated in replies." Respond as promptly and quickly as you can, but do not jump to a hasty, ill-considered answer.

11) Do not be peremptory in your answers

A brief answer is proper – but do not fire your answer back. That is a losing game from your point of view. The board member can probably ask questions much faster than you can answer them.

12) Do not try to create the answer you think the board member wants

He is interested in what kind of mind you have and how it works – not in playing games. Furthermore, he can usually spot this practice and will actually grade you down on it.

13) Do not switch sides in your reply merely to agree with a board member

Frequently, a member will take a contrary position merely to draw you out and to see if you are willing and able to defend your point of view. Do not start a debate, yet do not surrender a good position. If a position is worth taking, it is worth defending.

14) Do not be afraid to admit an error in judgment if you are shown to be wrong

The board knows that you are forced to reply without any opportunity for careful consideration. Your answer may be demonstrably wrong. If so, admit it and get on with the interview.

15) Do not dwell at length on your present job

The opening question may relate to your present assignment. Answer the question but do not go into an extended discussion. You are being examined for a *new* job, not your present one. As a matter of fact, try to phrase ALL your answers in terms of the job for which you are being examined.

Basis of Rating

Probably you will forget most of these "do's" and "don'ts" when you walk into the oral interview room. Even remembering them all will not ensure you a passing grade. Perhaps you did not have the qualifications in the first place. But remembering them will help you to put your best foot forward, without treading on the toes of the board members.

Rumor and popular opinion to the contrary notwithstanding, an oral board wants you to make the best appearance possible. They know you are under pressure – but they also want to see how you respond to it as a guide to what your reaction would be under the pressures of the job you seek. They will be influenced by the degree of poise you display, the personal traits you show and the manner in which you respond.

ABOUT THIS BOOK

This book contains tests divided into Examination Sections. Go through each test, answering every question in the margin. We have also attached a sample answer sheet at the back of the book that can be removed and used. At the end of each test look at the answer key and check your answers. On the ones you got wrong, look at the right answer choice and learn. Do not fill in the answers first. Do not memorize the questions and answers, but understand the answer and principles involved. On your test, the questions will likely be different from the samples. Questions are changed and new ones added. If you understand these past questions you should have success with any changes that arise. Tests may consist of several types of questions. We have additional books on each subject should more study be advisable or necessary for you. Finally, the more you study, the better prepared you will be. This book is intended to be the last thing you study before you walk into the examination room. Prior study of relevant texts is also recommended. NLC publishes some of these in our Fundamental Series. Knowledge and good sense are important factors in passing your exam. Good luck also helps. So now study this Passbook, absorb the material contained within and take that knowledge into the examination. Then do your best to pass that exam.

EXAMINATION SECTION

EXAMINATION SECTION
TEST 1

DIRECTIONS: Each question or incomplete statement is followed by several suggested answers or completions. Select the one that BEST answers the question or completes the statement. *PRINT THE LETTER OF THE CORRECT ANSWER IN THE SPACE AT THE RIGHT.*

1. An employee requests a book which is not in the department library. Of the following, the MOST advisable course of action for you to take is to 1.____

   A. attempt to get the book for him by means of the department's affiliation with the public library
   B. explain that the book is not available from the department's library
   C. suggest that he try his local public library and give him a list of local libraries
   D. tell him where he may purchase the book and offer to make the purchase for him

2. The catalog for the use of department employees has just been thoroughly checked and revised by a professional librarian. After trying to find the name of a book in the catalog, an employee tells you that he cannot find it. 2.____
   Of the following, the MOST advisable action for you to take FIRST is to

   A. call the public library for the exact title
   B. look it up in the catalog yourself
   C. look through the stacks for the book
   D. tell him you are sorry but the book is not in the department library

3. You find that three pages are missing from one of the copies of a very popular book in the department library. 3.____
   Of the following, the MOST advisable action for you to take is to

   A. discard the book since its usefulness is now sharply curtailed
   B. order another copy of the book but keep the old copy until the new one is received
   C. report the fact to the head of the department and request further instructions
   D. type copies of the pages from another volume of the book and tape them in the appropriate place

4. The department library is scheduled to close at 5 P.M. It is now 4:55, and an employee reading a book shows no signs of leaving. 4.____
   Of the following, the MOST advisable action for you to take is to

   A. tell him it is time to leave
   B. tell him the time and ask him if he wishes to borrow the book
   C. turn the lights off and on, indirectly suggesting that he leave
   D. wait until he decides to leave

5. The dealer from whom you have been buying books for the department library has informed you that henceforth he can give you only a fifteen percent instead of a twenty percent discount. 5.____
   Of the following, the MOST advisable course of action for you to take FIRST is to

A. accept the fifteen percent discount
B. inform the head of your department
C. investigate the discount given by other book dealers
D. order directly from the publishers

6. Your supervisor is a professional librarian and is responsible for the selection of material to be added to the department library in which you are an employee. Shortly after you start on the job, an employee of the department brings you a written request to have several books of his choice added to the library. 6.___
Of the following, the MOST advisable course of action for you to take is to

A. order the books immediately
B. pass the suggestion along to your supervisor
C. refuse to accept his suggestion
D. tell him that he will have to buy the books

7. You object to your supervisor's plan to change the system in the department library from closed to open stacks. 7.___
Of the following, the MOST advisable course of action for you to take is to

A. ask other members of the staff to support your objections
B. await further instructions and then do as you are told
C. discuss your objections with your supervisor
D. send a brief report of your objections to the department head

8. Two weeks after you begin working in the department library, you learn that books in library bindings last twice as long as those with the publishers' bindings. 8.___
Of the following, the MOST advisable course of action for you to follow is to

A. buy only paperbound books
B. have all new books put in library bindings
C. put in library bindings only rare editions
D. put in library bindings only those books likely to get hard use

9. Your superior is away on an official trip. You have been asked to type and e-mail several hundred letters before he returns. Just as you begin the job, the computer breaks down. 9.___
Of the following, the MOST advisable course of action for you to take is to

A. arrange to have the computer serviced as soon as possible
B. write the letters by hand
C. postpone the job until after your supervisor returns
D. write to your supervisor for advice

10. Your supervisor in the department library is out for the day. You receive a telephone call from another city department asking if they may borrow one of the books in your library. 10.___
Of the following, the MOST advisable action for you to take FIRST is to tell the department

A. that books are not permitted out of the department
B. that you will check and call back the next day
C. to send a representative to inquire the next day
D. to write a letter to the department head

11. Two months have passed since the head of the department has borrowed one of the books in the department library. Of the following, the MOST advisable action for you to take is to 11.____

A. ask the department head if he wishes to keep the book out longer
B. leave a note for the department head telling him that the book should be returned immediately
C. wait another month and then write the book off as lost
D. wait until you receive another request for the book

12. Your supervisor tells you that he would like to have all old book cards replaced, all torn pages mended, and the books put in good condition in all other respects by the following day. You know that this is an impossible task. 12.____
Of the following, the MOST advisable course of action for you to take is to

A. attempt to finish as much of the job as possible
B. explain the difficulties involved to the supervisor and await further instruction
C. ignore the request since it is completely unreasonable
D. make a complaint to the head of the department

13. The library in which you work has received about fifty new books. These books must be cataloged, but you have had no experience in this type of work. However, you have been told that a professional librarian will join the staff in about six weeks. 13.____
Of the following, the MOST advisable course of action for you to take in the meantime is to

A. close the library for a week and try to do the cataloging yourself
B. lend the books only to those who can get special permission
C. let the users take the books even though they are not cataloged
D. put all the books in storage until they can be cataloged

14. The hospital library in which you work has a large back-log of books that need to be mended. You are unable to do more than a small part of the job by yourself. One of the patients in the hospital has done book binding and mending. He offers to help you because he sees the need for doing the job and because he wants something to do with his hands. 14.____
Of the following, the MOST advisable course of action for you to take is to

A. accept his offer on condition that the doctor approves
B. ask him to push the book cart around the wards so you will be free to do the mending
C. refuse his offer
D. write a letter to his former employer to find out whether he is a good bookbinder

15. You accidentally spill a glass of water over an open book. 15.____
Of the following, the MOST advisable action for you to take FIRST in most cases is to

A. discard the book to prevent the water from spoiling other material
B. hang the book up by its binding
C. press the covers together to squeeze out the water
D. separate the wet pages with blotters

16. In mending a book, you overturn a jar of glue on a new book. 16.____
Of the following, the MOST advisable action for you to take FIRST is to

A. allow the glue to harden so that it may be peeled off
B. attempt to wipe off the glue with any clean scrap paper
C. discard the book to prevent other materials from being spoiled
D. report the incident immediately to your supervisor

17. Of the following, the situation LEAST likely to result in injury to books is one in which 17.____

A. all books support each other standing upright
B. short books are placed between tall ones
C. the books are as close together as possible
D. the books lean against the sides of the shelves

18. Of the following, a damp cloth may BEST be used to clean a cloth book cover that has been coated with 18.____

A. benzene
B. gold leaf
C. turpentine
D. varnish

19. Decay of leather bindings may be MOST effectively delayed by 19.____

A. a short tanning period
B. air conditioning
C. rubbing periodically with a damp cloth
D. treatment with heat

20. When paste is used to mend a page, it is MOST desirable that the page should then be 20.____

A. aired
B. heated
C. pressed
D. sprayed

21. A book that is perfectly clean but has been used by someone with chicken pox can probably BEST be handled by 21.____

A. burning, followed by proper disposal of the ashes
B. forty-eight hour exposure to ultraviolet light
C. keeping it out of circulation for six months
D. treating it the same as any other book

22. The BEST combination of temperature and humidity for books is temperature _______ degrees, humidity _______. 22.____

A. 50-60; 20-30%
B. 60-70; 10-20%
C. 60-70; 50-60%
D. 70-80; 70-80%

23. When a new book is received, it is LEAST important to keep a record of the 23.____

A. author's name
B. cost of the book
C. number of pages
D. source from which it was obtained

24. You have just received from the publisher a new book for the department library, but you find that the binding is torn. 24.____
Of the following, the MOST advisable action for you to take is to

A. mend the binding and take no further action
B. mend the binding but claim a price discount
C. report the damage to the department head
D. send the book back to the publisher

25. Of the following, a characteristic of MOST photographic charging systems is that 25.____

A. book cards are not used
B. charging is done by one person
C. date due is stamped on borrower's card
D. transaction cards are not used

KEY (CORRECT ANSWERS)

1. A
2. B
3. D
4. B
5. C
6. B
7. C
8. D
9. A
10. B
11. A
12. B
13. C
14. A
15. D
16. B
17. A
18. D
19. B
20. C
21. D
22. C
23. C
24. D
25. B

TEST 2

DIRECTIONS: Each question or incomplete statement is followed by several suggested answers or completions. Select the one that BEST answers the question or completes the statement. *PRINT THE LETTER OF THE CORRECT ANSWER IN THE SPACE AT THE RIGHT.*

1. In a card catalog, a reference from one subject heading to another is MOST commonly called a(n) _______ reference. 1._____

   A. cross B. direct C. primary D. indirect

2. A book which is shortened by omission of detail but which retains the general sense of the original is called a(n) 2._____

   A. compendium B. manuscript
   C. miniature D. abridgment

3. An anonymous book is a 3._____

   A. book published before 1500
   B. book whose author is unknown
   C. copy which is defective
   D. work that is out of print

4. All the letters, figures, and symbols assigned to a book to indicate its location on library shelves comprise the _______ number. 4._____

   A. call B. Cutter C. index D. inventory

5. The term *format* does NOT refer to a book's 5._____

   A. binding B. size
   C. theme D. typography

6. The term *card catalog* USUALLY refers to a 6._____

   A. catalog consisting of loose-leaf pages upon which the cards are pasted
   B. catalog in which entries are on separate cards arranged in a definite order
   C. catalog of the cards available from the Library of Congress
   D. record on cards of the works which have been weeded out of the library collection

7. The term *circulation record* USUALLY refers to a record of 7._____

   A. daily attendance
   B. the books borrowed
   C. the most popular books
   D. the books out on interlibrary loan

8. Reading shelves USUALLY involves checking the shelves to see that all the books 8._____

   A. are in the correct order
   B. are suitable for the library's patrons
   C. are there
   D. have been cataloged correctly

9. In an alphabetical catalog of book titles and authors' names, the name *de Santis* would be filed 9.____

   A. after *DeWitt*
   B. after *Sanders*
   C. before AND THEN THERE WERE NONE
   D. before *Deutsch*

10. In typing, the Shift key on the computer keyboard is used to 10.____

   A. change the font size
   B. indent a line of text
   C. type numbers
   D. type capitals

11. The abbreviation e.g. means *most nearly* 11.____

   A. as follows
   B. for example
   C. refer to
   D. that is

12. The abbreviation ff. means *most nearly* 12.____

   A. and following pages
   B. formerly
   C. frontispiece
   D. the end

13. The abbreviation ibid, means *most nearly* 13.____

   A. consult the index
   B. in the same place
   C. see below
   D. turn the page

14. *Ex libris* is a Latin phrase meaning 14.____

   A. former librarian
   B. from the books
   C. without charge
   D. without liberty

15. An expurgated edition of a book is one which 15.____

   A. contains many printing errors
   B. includes undesirable passages
   C. is not permitted in public libraries
   D. omits objectionable material

16. The re-charging of a book to a borrower is USUALLY called 16.____

   A. fining
   B. processing
   C. reissue
   D. renewal

17. A sheet of paper that is pierced with holes is 17.____

   A. borated
   B. collated
   C. perforated
   D. serrated

18. *Glossary* means *most nearly* a(n) 18.____

   A. dictionary of selected terms in a particular book or field
   B. list of chapter headings in the order in which they appear in a book
   C. section of the repairing division which coats books with a protective lacquer
   D. alphabetical table of the contents of a book

19. *Accessioning* means *most nearly* 19.____

A. acquiring books
B. arranging books for easy access
C. donating books as gifts
D. listing books in the order of purchase

20. *Bookplate* means *most nearly* 20.____

A. a label in a book showing who owns it
B. a metal device for holding books upright
C. a rounded zinc surface upon which a page is printed
D. the flat part of the binding of a book

21. *Thesaurus* means *most nearly* a book which 21.____

A. contains instructions on how to prepare a thesis
B. contains words grouped according to similarity of meaning
C. describes the techniques of dramatic acting
D. gives quotations from well-known works of literature

22. *Salacious* means *most nearly* 22.____

A. careful B. delicious C. lewd D. salty

23. *Pseudonym* means *most nearly* 23.____

A. false report
B. fictitious name
C. libelous statement
D. psychic phenomenon

24. *Gamut* means *most nearly* a(n) 24.____

A. bookworm
B. simpleton
C. vagrant
D. entire range

25. *Monograph* means *most nearly* a 25.____

A. machine for duplicating typewritten material by means of a stencil
B. picture reproduced on an entire page of a manuscript
C. single chart used to represent statistical data
D. systematic treatise on a particular subject

KEY (CORRECT ANSWERS)

1.	A	11.	B
2.	D	12.	A
3.	B	13.	B
4.	A	14.	B
5.	C	15.	D
6.	B	16.	D
7.	B	17.	C
8.	A	18.	A
9.	D	19.	D
10.	D	20.	A

21.	B
22.	C
23.	B
24.	D
25.	D

TEST 3

DIRECTIONS: Each question or incomplete statement is followed by several suggested answers or completions. Select the one that BEST answers the question or completes the statement. *PRINT THE LETTER OF THE CORRECT ANSWER IN THE SPACE AT THE RIGHT.*

Questions 1-15.

DIRECTIONS: Questions 1 through 15 are to be answered SOLELY on the basis of the information contained in the following passage.

Machines may be useful for bibliographic purposes, but they will be useful only if we study the bibliographic requirements to be met and the machines available, in terms of each Job which needs to be done. Many standard tools now available are more efficient than high-speed machines if the machines are used as gadgets rather than as the mechanical elements of well-considered systems.

It does not appear impossible for us to learn to think in terms of scientific management to such an extent that we may eventually be able to do much of the routine part of bibliographic work mechanically with greater efficiency, both in terms of cost per unit of service and in terms of management of the intellectual content of literature. There are many bibliographic tasks which will probably not be done mechanically in the near future because the present tools appear to present great advantages over any machine in sight; for example, author bibliography done on the electronic machines would appear to require almost as much work in instructing the machine as is required to look in an author catalog. The major field of usefulness of the machines would appear to be that of subject bibliography, and particularly in research rather than quick reference jobs.

Machines now available or in sight cannot answer a quick reference question either as fast or as economically as will consultation of standard reference works such as dictionaries, encyclopedias, or almanacs, nor would it appear worthwhile to instruct a machine and run the machine to pick out one recent book or "any recent book" in a broad subject field. It would appear, therefore, that high-speed electronic or electrical machinery may be used for bibliographic purposes only in research institutions, at least for the next five or ten years, and their use will probably be limited to research problems in those institutions. It seems quite probable that during the next decade electronic machines, including the Rapid Selector, which was designed with bibliographic purposes in mind, will find application in administrative, office, and business uses to a much greater extent than they will in bibliographic operations.

The shortcomings of machines used as gadgets have been stressed in this paper. Nevertheless, the use of machines for bibliographic purposes is developing, and it is developing rapidly. It appears quite certain that several of the machines and mechanical devices can now perform certain of the routine operations involved in bibliographic work more accurately and more efficiently than these operations can be performed without them.

At least one machine, the Rapid Selector, appears potentially capable of performing higher orders of bibliographic work than we have been able to perform in the past, if and when we learn: (a) what is really needed for the advancement of learning in the way of bibliographic services; and (b) how to utilize the machine efficiently.

There is no magic in machines as such. There will be time-lag in their application, just as there was with the typewriter. The speed and efficiency in handling the mechanical part of bibliographic work, which will determine the point of diminishing returns, depend in large measure on how long it will be before we approach these problems from the point of view of scientific management.

This report cannot solve the problem of bibliographic organization. Machines alone cannot solve the problem. We need to develop systems of handling the mass of bibliographic material, but such systems cannot be developed until we discover and establish our objectives, our plans, our standards, our methods and controls, within the framework of each situation. This may take twenty years or it may take one hundred, but it will come. The termination of how long the time-lag will be rests upon our time-lag in gathering objective information upon which scientific management of literature can be based.

1. On the basis of the above passage, machines will *probably* be MOST useful in 1.____

   A. determining the cost per unit of service
   B. quick reference jobs
   C. subject bibliography
   D. title cataloging

2. On the basis of the above passage, the Rapid Selector will *probably* be LEAST used during the next ten years in 2.____

   A. administration
   B. bibliographic work
   C. business
   D. office work

3. It may be inferred from the above passage that is is NOT practical to use machines to do author bibliography because 3.____

   A. experienced machine operators are not available
   B. more than one machine is needed for such a task
   C. the results obtained from a machine are unreliable
   D. too much work is involved in instructing the machine

4. On the basis of the above passage, one of the criteria of efficiency is the 4.____

   A. amount of work required
   B. cost per unit of service
   C. net cost of service
   D. number of machines available

5. On the basis of the above passage, the LEAST efficient of the following for quick reference jobs are 5.____

   A. bibliographies
   B. dictionaries
   C. encyclopedias
   D. machines

6. On the basis of the above passage, in the next few years, high-speed electronic machinery will probably be used for bibliographic purposes only by 6.____

   A. civil engineers
   B. institutions of higher education
   C. publishers
   D. research institutions

7. On the basis of the above passage, the Rapid Selector was designed for use in handling 7.____

A. bibliographic operations
B. computing problems
C. photographic reproduction
D. standard reference works

8. On the basis of the above passage, progress on the development of machines to do bibliographic tasks has reached the point at which 8.____

A. all present tools have become obsolete
B. certain jobs are better performed with machines than without them
C. machines are as efficient in doing quick reference jobs as in doing special research jobs
D. machines are no longer regarded as being too expensive

9. The one of the following which is NOT stated by the above passage to be essential in developing ways of handling bibliographic material is 9.____

A. discovering methods and controls
B. establishing objectives
C. establishing standards
D. obtaining historical data

10. The above passage indicates that machines alone will NOT be able to solve the problem of 10.____

A. bibliographic organization
B. reference work
C. scientific management
D. system analysis

11. On the basis of the above passage, the viewpoint of scientific management is essential in 11.____

A. developing the mechanical handling of bibliographic work
B. operating the Rapid Selector
C. repairing electronic machines
D. showing that people are always superior to machines in bibliographic work

12. On the basis of the above passage, there are machines in existence which 12.____

A. are particularly useful for statistical analysis in library work
B. are the result of scientific management of bibliographic work
C. have not been efficiently utilized for bibliographic work
D. may be installed in a medium-sized library

13. On the basis of the above passage, the scientific management of literature awaits the 13.____

A. assembling of objective information
B. compilation of new reference books
C. development of more complex machines
D. development of simplified machinery

14. Based on the above passage, it may be INFERRED that the author's attitude toward the use of machines in bibliographic work is that they 14.____

    A. have limited usefulness at the present time
    B. will become useful only if scientific management is applied
    C. will probably always be restricted to routine operations
    D. will probably never be useful

15. The author of the above passage believes that high-speed machines are BEST adapted to bibliographic work when they are used 15.____

    A. as gadgets
    B. in place of standard reference works
    C. to perform complex operations
    D. to perform routine operations

Questions 16-25.

DIRECTIONS: Questions 16 through 25 deal with the classification of non-fiction books according to the Dewey Classification as outlined below. For each book listed, print in the space on the right the letter in front of the class to which it belongs.

	Classification	
16. Ernst. WORDS: ENGLISH ROOTS AND HOW THEY GROW	A. 000 General Works	16.____
17. Faulkner. FROM VERSAILLES TO THE NEW DEAL	B. 100 Philosophy	17.____
18. Fry. CHINESE ART	C. 200 Religion	18.____
19. Kant. CRITIQUE OF PURE REASON	D. 300 Social Science	19.____
20. Millikan. THE ELECTRON	E. 400 Philology	20.____
21. Morgan. THEORY OF THE GENE	F. 500 Pure Science	21.____
22. Raine. THE YEAR ONE; POEMS	G. 600 Applied Science, Useful Arts	22.____
23. Richards. PRINCIPLES OF LITERARY CRITICISM	H. 700 Fine Arts	23.____
24. Steinberg. BASIC JUDAISM	I. 800 Literature, Belleslettres	24.____
25. Strachey. QUEEN VICTORIA	J. 900 History, Biography	25.____

KEY (CORRECT ANSWERS)

1. C
2. B
3. D
4. B
5. D
6. D
7. A
8. B
9. D
10. A
11. A
12. C
13. A
14. A
15. D
16. E
17. J
18. H
19. B
20. F
21. F
22. I
23. I
24. C
25. J

EXAMINATION SECTION

TEST 1

DIRECTIONS: Each question or incomplete statement is followed by several suggested answers or completions. Select the one that BEST answers the question or completes the statement. *PRINT THE LETTER OF THE CORRECT ANSWER IN THE SPACE AT THE RIGHT.*

Questions 1-5.

DIRECTIONS: Arrange the following names in alphabetical order as they would appear on the hold shelf of a library by matching the name in Column A with its order position in Column B.

Column A	Column B	
1. Smiles, Roy	A. First	1.____
	B. Second	
2. Smigel, Robert	C. Third	2.____
	D. Fourth	
3. Smith, Raymond	E. Fifth	3.____
4. Smith, Rhonda		4.____
5. Smiegel, Rayna		5.____

Questions 6-10.

DIRECTIONS: Each of Questions 6 through 10 may be:
A. Incorrect due to improper spelling
B. Incorrect due to improper punctuation
C. Incorrect due to improper capitalization
D. Correct

6. The reference section is non-circulating, this means you can't check these items out. 6.____

7. The book can be found in the non-ficton section of the library. 7.____

8. Biographies are a popular selection among all age groups at our library. 8.____

9. The elm grove library is the third biggest library in the county. 9.____

10. Since your book was one week overdue, I cannot wave this fine for you. 10.____

Questions 11-15.

DIRECTIONS: Questions 11 through 15 are to be answered SOLELY on the basis of the information given in the following paragraph.

Libraries have a long history, with the oldest recorded library dating back to Ancient Egypt circa 367 BC to 283 BC. In recent years, however, technological developments have changed the nature of library service. The rise of the internet and the growing number of digital libraries have resulted in a decrease in library usage. Throughout history, library service has primarily focused on the collection of books and other resources a library offers to its patrons. This collection-centered approach to library service has been challenged by the public's ability to access much of this information virtually without ever stepping inside of a library. Fortunately, there is another approach to library service that remains useful and relevant in the digital age: a user-centered approach. A user-centered approach shifts the focus from a library's physical collection to the services it provides to promote learning and social interaction among its users.

11. Based on what you've read in the above paragraph, which of the following would be an example of user-centered library service? 11.____
    A. A library's acquisition of a rare manuscript
    B. The expansion of a library's digital collection
    C. The installation of more shelving to house a larger and more diverse collection
    D. the creation of a librarian-led study group for adult learners returning to school

12. According to the above paragraph, libraries have been around for about _____ years. 12.____
    A. 500 B. 2,300 C. 1,700 D. 100

13. According to the above paragraph, what has made a collection-centered approach to library service less useful? 13.____
    A. Poor collection development B. A decrease in book prices
    C. Technological advancements D. A more educated public

14. Based on what you've read in the above paragraph, what must libraries do to remain relevant in the modern age? 14.____
    A. Adopt a user-centered approach to library service
    B. Adopt a collection-centered approach to library service
    C. Seek funding from new sources
    D. Abandon physical collections for completely digital collections

15. Based on what you've read in the above paragraph, which of the following BEST describes the difference between collection-centered and user-centered library service? 15.____
    Collection-centered library service focuses on _____, while user-centered library service focuses on _____.
    A. the services a library offers that promote learning and socialization; a library's physical holdings of books and resources
    B. digitizing a library's entire collection; maintaining a physical collection

C. maintaining a physical collection; digitizing a library's entire collection
D. a library's physical holdings of books and resources; the services a library offers that promote learning and socialization

Questions 16-20.

DIRECTIONS: Questions 16 through 20 each consist of four call numbers in Column A and Column B. Compare the numbers listed in each column and use the following to provide your answer:
A. One call number in Column A and Column B are the same
B. Two call numbers in Column A and Column B are the same
C. Three call numbers in Column A and Column B are the same
D. All four call numbers in Column A and Column B are the same

	Column A	Column B	
16.	696.45 BAC 645.96 CAB 656.46 DAN 646.56 AND	696.45 CAB 645.96 BAC 656.46 DAN 646.56 AND	16.____
17.	251.84 NEJ 258.14 ENE 284.84 NEE 248.15 JEE	251.84 NEJ 258.14 ENE 284.84 NEE 248.15 JEE	17.____
18.	199.33 WEN 139.93 WEW 113.31 NEW 133.99 WEE	199.33 WEN 139.93 WEN 113.31 WEW 133.93 WEE	18.____
19.	823.65 HOW 832.56 WHO 862.35 WOW 856.23 WON	823.65 HOW 823.56 WHO 862.35 WOW 856.23 WON	19.____
20.	429.55 BEB 495.22 BEE 422.95 EBB 492.59 EBE	429.55 BEB 492.22 BEE 422.95 EBB 495.29 EBE	20.____

Questions 21-25.

DIRECTIONS: Questions 21 through 25 are to be answered on the basis of the following table.

Dry Creek Library Monthly Adult Program Records				
Program	Number of Attendees Ages 18-24	Number of Attendees Ages 25-44	Number of Attendees Ages 45-65	Number of Attendees Age 65+
Writers' Group	4	5	4	3
Knitting Circle	4	3	3	2
Tai Chi	3	4	1	6
Mystery Book Club	0	2	3	4
Non-Fiction Book Club	2	5	4	3

21. Which program has the HIGHEST attendance rate? 21.____
    A. Writers' Group
    B. Tai Chi
    C. Non-Fiction Book Club
    D. Knitting Circle

22. Which age group has the HIGHEST participation rate in monthly library programs? 22.____
    A. 18-24
    B. 25-44
    C. 45-65
    D. 65+

23. Which program is MOST popular among 18 to 44 year olds? 23.____
    A. Writers' Group
    B. Knitting Club
    C. Mystery Book Club
    D. Non-Fiction Book Club

24. If the library were to discontinue a program, which program would be the MOST logical choice based upon these program records? 24.____
    A. Writers' Group
    B. Tai Chi
    C. Mystery Book Club
    D. Knitting Circle

25. If the library wants to expand one program from monthly to weekly in order to attract more seniors, which program would be the MOST logical choice based on these program records? 25.____
    A. Writers' Group
    B. Knitting Circle
    C. Mystery Book Club
    D. Tai Chi

KEY (CORRECT ANSWERS)

1. C
2. B
3. D
4. E
5. A

6. B
7. A
8. D
9. C
10. A

11. D
12. B
13. C
14. A
15. D

16. B
17. D
18. A
19. C
20. B

21. A
22. B
23. A
24. C
25. D

TEST 2

DIRECTIONS: Each question or incomplete statement is followed by several suggested answers or completions. Select the one that BEST answers the question or completes the statement. *PRINT THE LETTER OF THE CORRECT ANSWER IN THE SPACE AT THE RIGHT.*

1. Which of the following words is spelled INCORRECTLY? 1.____
   A. microfiche B. photocopyer C. interlibrary D. catalog

2. Which of the following sentences includes an error in punctuation? 2.____
   A. I'm holding Mr. Rutgers book at the circulation desk.
   B. All meeting rooms are currently reserved.
   C. Only library cardholders can request books through interlibrary loan.
   D. Children's books are located upstairs in the Youth Services Department.

3. Which of the following sentences includes a capitalization error? 3.____
   A. The library director must sign off on all purchases.
   B. This week the Ashton Public Library Book Club is reading *The Paris Wife*.
   C. If you need help with academic research, you should speak with a librarian in the department of reference services.
   D. Our most popular program is our weekly Gourmet Club, where people come together to talk about fine food and drinks.

4. Which of the following words is spelled INCORRECTLY? 4.____
   A. biography B. anthology C. magizine D. bibliography

5. Which of the following sentences includes an error in punctuation? 5.____
   A. Can I see your driver's license?
   B. Ms. Janda said that she would be arriving 10 minutes late for the computer class.
   C. There are only three copies left of the book selected for the monthly book club.
   D. Who did you speak to over the phone about this hold request.

Questions 6-10.

DIRECTIONS: Questions 6 through 10 include sentences with one word underlined. For each question, please select the word with the CLOSEST meaning to the underlined word.

6. Mr. Banks has a block on his account because he has too many <u>fines</u>. 6.____
   A. charges B. items C. warnings D. restrictions

7. *The Girl With the Dragon Tattoo* received overwhelmingly positive <u>reviews</u>. 7.____
   A. investments B. reassessments
   C. critiques D. inspections

8. When you write a research paper, you must include <u>citations</u>. 8.____
   A. commendations B. references
   C. facts D. inferences

9. If you make a copy of that CD, you are <u>infringing</u> upon copyright law. 9.____
   A. preserving B. misunderstanding
   C. violating D. elucidating

10. *Architectural Digest* is located on the first floor with the other <u>serials</u>. 10.____
    A. books B. databases C. periodicals D. archives

Questions 11-15.

DIRECTIONS: Questions 11 through 15 consist of four addresses in Column A and Column B. Compare the addresses listed in each column and use the following to provide your answer:
A. One address in Column A and Column B are the same.
B. Two addresses in Column A and Column B are the same.
C. Three addresses in Column A and Column B are the same.
D. All four addresses in Column A and Column B are the same.

	Column A	Column B	
11.	3941 Blackwell Dr. 3491 Blackwell Dr. 3991 Blackswell St. 3945 Blackstreet Ave.	3941 Blackwell Dr. 3914 Balckwell Dr. 3941 Blackwell St. 3945 Blackstreet Dr.	11.____
12.	204 Rhodes Ave. Apt. B 206 Rhodes Ave. Apt. 6 206 Rhoades Ave. Apt B 260 Rhodes St. Apt. B6	204 Rhodes Ave. Apt. B 204 Rhodes Ave. Apt 4 206 Rhoades Ave. Apt. B 260 Rhodes St. Apt. B6	12.____
13.	1155 Judith Rd. 1515 Judith Ln. 5111 Judy Rd. 1155 Judy Ln.	1155 Judith Rd. 1515 Judith Ln. 5111 Judy Rd. 1155 Judy Ln.	13.____
14.	2367 Cascade Blvd. 7632 Cascade Ave. 2367 Cascadia Blvd. 7632 Cascade Blvd.	2376 Cascade Blvd. 7632 Cascade Ave. 2367 Cascadia Blvd. 7632 Cascadia Blvd.	14.____
15.	106 Brooks Ln. Apt. 12 102 Brooks Ln. Apt. 16 126 Brook Ln. Apt. 11 162 Brook Ave. Apt. 2	106 Brooks Ln. Apt. 12 102 Brooks Ln. Apt. 16 126 Brooks Ln. Apt. 11 166 Brook Ave. Apt. 2	15.____

Questions 16-20.

DIRECTIONS: In Questions 16 through 20, please match the author's last name in Column A with its proper order on the shelf of a library that organizes fiction alphabetically by author's last name in Column B.

Column A	Column B	
16. Brockenstein	A. First	16.____
	B. Second	
17. Brock	C. Third	17.____
	D. Fourth	
18. Broadchurch	E. Fifth	18.____
19. Broadbent		19.____
20. Brockley		20.____

21. If a patron returns five books two days past their due date, and overdue charges accrue at 15 cents per day for each book, how much does the patron owe in overdue fees? 21.____
    A. $1.50 B. $0.75 C. $3.00 D. $5.75

22. Susan is compiling statistics from monthly library usage records. Records state that over the course of one month, patrons checked out 5,375 adult fiction titles, 4,789 adult non-fiction titles, 6,854 audio-visual items, and 3,632 magazines. Based on these records, fiction titles comprise about _____ percent of overall monthly circulation. 22.____
    A. 52 B. 26 C. 15 D. 38

23. Yearly statistics show that over the course of one week an average of 33 patrons attend library programs. If there are four programs scheduled during one week, about how many patrons will be attending each program? 23.____
    A. 3 B. 11 C. 5 D. 8

24. Jane is calling patrons to inform them that the interlibrary loan books they requested have arrived. It takes Jane approximately five minutes to notify each patron, and she has a cart filled with 37 interlibrary books that require patron notification. She also has a bin full of returned books that need to be checked in and shelved. How long will it take Jane to finish the hold notifications so she can move on to her next task? 24.____
    A. One hour B. About six hours
    C. About three hours D. 45 minutes

25. Birch Grove Library has a rule that patrons can only check out 50 books at a time, 50 audio-visual items at a time, and 15 interlibrary loan items at a time. The library also has a rule that no more than 75 items total can be checked out to a patron's account at one time. If a patron already has 45 books, 25 audio-visual items, and 5 interlibrary loan items checked out, she can 25.____
   A. still check out 5 books, 25 audio-visual items, 5 interlibrary loan items
   B. no longer check anything out until she returns some of her items
   C. still check out 30 books
   D. still check out 10 interlibrary loan items and 25 audio-visual items

KEY (CORRECT ANSWERS)

1.	B	11.	A
2.	A	12.	C
3.	C	13.	D
4.	C	14.	B
5.	D	15.	B
6.	A	16.	D
7.	C	17.	C
8.	B	18.	B
9.	C	19.	A
10.	C	20.	E

21.	A
22.	B
23.	D
24.	C
25.	B

TEST 3

DIRECTIONS: Each question or incomplete statement is followed by several suggested answers or completions. Select the one that BEST answers the question or completes the statement. *PRINT THE LETTER OF THE CORRECT ANSWER IN THE SPACE AT THE RIGHT.*

Questions 1-5.

DIRECTIONS: Questions 1 through 5 are to be answered on the basis of the following paragraph.

Copyright law plays an important role in how libraries operate and provide information to their patrons. Libraries must abide by state and federal copyright laws, including the Copyright Act, which is the most authoritative source of copyright law in the United States. Through the Copyright Act's first sale doctrine, libraries are allowed to lend books and other copyrighted material. Additionally, the Copyright Act's fair use law allows library patrons to use copyrighted materials for specific functions, such as criticism, comment, news reporting, scholarship, and research. Copyright law also allows libraries to reproduce copyrighted works in order to preserve or replace these works or provide them to people with disabilities.

1. Which of the following would NOT be an acceptable reason for a library to reproduce copyrighted material? 1.____
   A. To deliver it to a person who is housebound due to a physical disability
   B. To sell it in the library's book sale in order to raise funds for the library's remodel
   C. To preserve a book that is currently out of print and that also has limited used copies available
   D. To replace a copy of a rare book that has been lost

2. Which law allows libraries to lend books and other copyrighted materials? 2.____
   A. This is not allowed under state or federal law
   B. The fair use law
   C. The first sale doctrine
   D. The first use act

3. Based on the fair use law, libraries can allow patrons to quote or use passages from copyrighted materials in 3.____
   A. newspaper articles
   B. business brochures
   C. book manuscripts set for publication
   D. television advertisements

4. In the United States, copyright law PRIMARILY comes from 4.____
   A. state law
   B. the first use act
   C. municipal law
   D. the Copyright Act

5. The fair use law can be found in 5.____
A. state law
B. the Copyright Act
C. the First Amendment
D. municipal law

6. Which of the following words is spelled INCORRECTLY? 6.____
A. alamnac B. dictionary C. atlas D. encyclopedia

7. Which of the following sentences contains an error in punctuation? 7.____
A. There are two titles on hold for members of the library's book club: *Gone Girl* and *Me Before You*.
B. At the beginning of each month the library director holds a staff meeting that everyone is required to attend.
C. Did you ask the patron for her photo I.D. before providing her with her account information?
D. The library's Knitting Circle meets the first Thursday, second Saturday and third Monday of every month.

8. Which of the following words is spelled INCORRECTLY? 8.____
A. classification B. plagarism C. withdrawn D. volume

9. Which of the following sentences includes an error in capitalization? 9.____
A. All of the items you had on hold were sent back Tuesday.
B. Did Mr. Phekos register for this week's cooking demonstration?
C. Tanner is helping with the fundraiser because he is a member of the friends of the library.
D. Book donations can be placed in the donation box near the circulation desk.

10. Which of the following words is spelled INCORRECTLY? 10.____
A. thesarus B. thesis C. series D. reserve

Questions 11-15.

DIRECTIONS: Questions 11 through 15 each contain three lines of letters in Column A and three lines of numbers in Column B. The letters in each line should correspond with the numbers in each line as outlined in the following table:

Letter	J	R	D	T	M	C	P	K	O	S
Matching Number	0	1	2	3	4	5	6	7	8	9

Please answer the questions as follows:
A. None of the lines of letters and lines of numbers are matched correctly.
B. One of the lines of letters and numbers is matched correctly.
C. Two of the lines of letters and lines of numbers are matched correctly.
D. All three of the lines of letters and lines of numbers are matched correctly.

	Column A	Column B	
11.	JMCP RMKS CPRO	0456 1479 5618	11.____
12.	DRKS MKPJ JDCP	9172 4761 0256	12.____
13.	CSDJ RKRD JKPC	5924 1712 0765	13.____
14.	TMMO CPDR JOTS	3448 5632 0839	14.____
15.	JCMS ROST MKJD	0648 1983 4701	15.____

Questions 16-20.

DIRECTIONS: In Questions 16 through 20, match the book title in Column A with its proper alphabetical orders based on letter by letter filing rules.

	Column A	Column B	
16.	To Kill a Mockingbird	A. First B. Second	16.____
17.	A Tale of Two Cities	C. Third D. Fourth	17.____
18.	The Time Traveler's Wife	E. Fifth	18.____
19.	Treasure Island		19.____
20.	The Two Towers		20.____

Questions 21-25.

DIRECTIONS: Questions 21 through 25 are to be answered on the basis of the following table.

Dry Creek Library 2023 Library Card Registration by Season					
Season	Number of Registrants Under 18	Number of Registrants Ages 18-24	Number of Registrants Ages 25-44	Number of Registrants Ages 45-65	Number of Registrants Age 65+
Winter	56	34	69	48	34
Spring	72	47	55	62	48
Summer	100	75	71	89	101
Fall	96	115	88	72	63

21. During which season does Dry Creek Library experience the MOST library card registrations? 21.____
    A. Winter B. Spring C. Summer D. Fall

22. Which of the following age groups registered for the MOST library cards in 2023? 22.____
    A. Under 18 B. 18-24 C. 25-44 D. 45-65

23. Which of the following patrons is MOST likely to register for a library card in the fall based on the data shown in the above table? 23.____
    A. A 10-year-old preparing for the new school year
    B. A 65-year-old who has just retired from his full-time job
    C. An 18-year-old entering her first semester of college
    D. A 26-year-old enrolled in medical school

24. During which season should Dry Creek Library increase marketing efforts to draw in more registrants between the ages of 18 and 24? 24.____
    A. Winter B. Spring C. Summer D. Fall

25. In 2022, 1,364 people registered for new library cards. How does this number compare to the number of registrants in 2023? 25.____
    It is _____ registered in 2023.
    A. the same amount of people that
    B. slightly less than the number of people who
    C. significantly more than the number of people who
    D. significantly less than the number of people who

KEY (CORRECT ANSWERS)

1. B
2. C
3. A
4. D
5. B

6. A
7. B
8. B
9. C
10. A

11. D
12. B
13. C
14. C
15. A

16. C
17. A
18. B
19. D
20. E

21. C
22. A
23. C
24. A
25. B

TEST 4

DIRECTIONS: Each question or incomplete statement is followed by several suggested answers or completions. Select the one that BEST answers the question or completes the statement. *PRINT THE LETTER OF THE CORRECT ANSWER IN THE SPACE AT THE RIGHT.*

Questions 1-5.

DIRECTIONS: Each of the sentences provided in Questions 1 through 5 may be:
A. Incorrect due to improper spelling
B. Incorrect due to improper punctuation
C. Incorrect due to improper capitalization
D. Correct

1. When you search the library's catalog online you can search by author, title, subject or, keyword. 1.____

2. The movie "Ghostbusters" is available on DVD or Blu-Ray in the library's audiovisual department. 2.____

3. The library hosts a group for writers that meets monthly and a children's story hour that meets weekly. 3.____

4. Reference librarians are best equipped to answer questions about the library's electronic resorces. 4.____

5. Library patrons can sign into their library account online to pay fines, rezerve books and check their due dates. 5.____

Questions 6-10.

DIRECTIONS: Questions 6 through 10 include sentences with one word underlined. Please select the word with the CLOSEST meaning to the underlined word.

6. The patron has <u>requested</u> that the book be held for an extra two days because she is on vacation. 6.____
A. refused B. asked C. determined D. stated

7. The Oak Creek Village Library participates in a <u>reciprocal</u> borrowing program in which it shares library materials with 25 other libraries. 7.____
A. individual B. restrictive
C. collaborative D. bibliographic

8. In libraries, books are assigned a call number based upon the book's <u>subject</u>. 8.____
A. title B. author C. chronology D. topic

9. Every year, the library director and board of directors review and update library <u>policies</u>. 9.____
   A. procedures B. collections C. events D. affairs

10. Librarians at the Poplar Lane Library are sometimes asked to <u>proctor</u> official tests and exams. 10.____
   A. barter B. supervise C. process D. create

Questions 11-15.

DIRECTIONS: In answering Questions 11 through 15, arrange the following names in alphabetical order as they would appear on the hold shelf of a library by matching the name in Column A with its order position in Column B.

	Column A	Column B	
11.	Frey, James	A. First	11.____
		B. Second	
12.	Friend, Jayne	C. Third	12.____
		D. Fourth	
13.	Frye, Jada	E. Fifth	13.____
14.	Friel, Jewel		14.____
15.	Frillo, Juno		15.____

Questions 16-20.

DIRECTIONS: Questions 16 through 20 each consist of four call numbers in Column A and Column B. Compare the numbers listed in each column and use the following to provide your answer:
A. One call number in Column A and Column B are the same.
B. Two call numbers in Column A and Column B are the same.
C. Three call numbers in Column A and Column B are the same.
D. All four call numbers in Column A and Column B are the same.

	Column A	Column B	
16.	147.74CAL	147.74CAL	16.____
	174.47LAC	174.44LAC	
	144.77LAL	177.44LAL	
	411.77CAC	477.11CAL	
17.	467.09DAN	467.09DAN	17.____
	469.07DAD	469.07DAD	
	460.79NAD	460.79NAD	
	468.32DAJ	468.23DAJ	

18. 219.57KAR 219.57KAR 18.____
215.97KAR 215.57KAR
257.19RAR 257.19RAR
275.19KAK 275.19KAK

19. 112.48PAU 112.58PAU 19.____
112.85PUA 112.85PUA
124.18PUL 124.18PUL
142.85PAU 142.85PAA

20. 102.75CHR 102.75CHR 20.____
175.27CRI 175.27CRI
107.25CHR 107.25CHR
157.22CRI 157.22CRI

21. Old Towne Library is hosting a speaking event and book signing with a well-known author. Seats are available for 120 people, but the author only has one hour to sign books afterward. If it takes about three minutes to sign each person's book, how many of the event's attendees will be able to participate in the book signing? 21.____
A. All of them B. 20 C. 100 D. 50

22. If Fleetwood Library owns a total of 1,000 DVDs (500 in the fiction section and 500 in the non-fiction section), how many DVDs would the library have left if the library director decided to withdraw 120 fiction DVDs and 150 non-fiction DVDs, while simultaneously adding 75 fiction DVDs and 60 non-fiction DVDs? 22.____
A. 730 B. 805 C. 865 D. 950

23. Tandy has been asked to create the schedule for the circulation staff at Morton Pass Library. The library is open from 10 A.M. to 9 P.M. Monday through Friday, from 10 A.M. to 5 P.M. on Saturday, and from 12 P.M. to 5 P.M. on Sunday. The library director requires that two staff members work at the desk during all hours of operation. What is the TOTAL number of hours Tandy will need to schedule staff for next week's schedule? 23.____
A. 134 B. 55 C. 201 D. 68

24. The Boynton Canyon Library hosts a weekly book discussion group every Thursday night. If 8 people attended the group the first week of February, 11 attended the second week, 7 attended the third week, and 10 attended the fourth week, what is the average number of attendees for the month of February? 24.____
A. 9 B. 34 C. 10 D. 7

25. A library patron has $6.60 in fines on his library account. He returns five more books five days late and is charged $.15 a day for each book. The library does not let patrons check out library materials when the fines on their account exceed $10.00. Which of the following statements BEST describes the patron's current situation? 25.____
The patron
   A. has less than $10.00 in fines and can still check out library materials
   B. must pay at least $1.00 in fines before he can check out more library materials
   C. must pay at least $.60 in fines before he can check out more library materials
   D. must pay at least $.35 in fines before he can check out more library materials

---

KEY (CORRECT ANSWERS)

1.	B	11.	A
2.	C	12.	C
3.	D	13.	E
4.	A	14.	B
5.	A	15.	D
6.	B	16.	A
7.	C	17.	C
8.	D	18.	C
9.	A	19.	B
10.	B	20.	D

21.	B
22.	C
23.	A
24.	A
25.	D

EXAMINATION SECTION
TEST 1

DIRECTIONS: Each question or incomplete statement is followed by several suggested answers or completions. Select the one that BEST answers the question or completes the statement. *PRINT THE LETTER OF THE CORRECT ANSWER IN THE SPACE AT THE RIGHT.*

1. A library is in the process of conducting an annual performance evaluation. Which of the following would be an output measure that might be used in this process? 1.____

   A. Staff expenditures
   B. User satisfaction survey results
   C. Ratio of computer workstations to daily average users
   D. Ratio of interlibrary loan lending to borrowing

2. The ______ record is a separate record attached to the bibliographic record for a serial title in which the receipt of individual issues or parts is entered on an ongoing basis. 2.____

   A. holdings
   B. check-in
   C. item
   D. periodical

3. Of the following, which research tool would be most appropriate for finding where an author uses specific words or phrases? 3.____

   A. Abstract
   B. Gazetteer
   C. Dictionary
   D. Concordance

4. In library cataloging, a separately published part of a bibliographic resource, usually representing a subject category within the whole and indicated by a topical heading or an alphanumeric heading, is a(n) 4.____

   A. class
   B. scope
   C. notch
   D. section

5. The main advantage to paying an electronic journal publisher on a per-article basis, rather than subscribing to a package or database, is that 5.____

   A. hardware, browser, and networking requirements are simpler
   B. the library pays only for what it uses
   C. costs are shifted entirely to the user
   D. costs are more predictable over time

6. The Dublin Core Metadata Initiative, an international effort to develop standard mechanisms for searching online resources, has named 15 core metadata elements to be used to direct searches. Which of the following is NOT one of these? 6.____

   A. Editor B. Rights C. Date D. Format

7. "Converting" electronic records means that 7.___

   A. there is a change to the underlying bit stream, but there is no change in the representation or intellectual content of the records
   B. they are moved from a proprietary legacy system that lacks software functionality to an open system
   C. they have been transferred from old storage media to new storage media with the same format specifications and without any loss in structure, content, or context
   D. they have been exported or imported from one software environment to another without the loss of structure, content, or context even though the underlying bit stream has likely been altered

8. The 3XX fields in the MARC system contain 8.___

   A. physical descriptions
   B. main entries
   C. subject added entries
   D. titles, editions, and imprints

9. In Internet user, instead of being taken to a desired Web page, instead is taken to a page that says *Error Message 404.* What has happened? 9.___

   A. Either the server is busy, or the site has moved.
   B. Special permission is needed to access the site.
   C. The file has been moved or deleted, or the URL in incorrect.
   D. The syntax used in the URL is incorrect.

10. An anthology is compiled by 6 authors. According to the MLA format, how many of the author's names should be included in a citation? 10.___

   A. 0
   B. 1
   C. 2
   D. 6

11. Which of the following is NOT an advantage of using HTML as a format for file preservation? 11.___

   A. Extensive authoring tools
   B. Improving tools for conversion-to-HTML
   C. Good standard for delivering simple text
   D. Can be viewed in any browser

12. In the MARC record, the same digits are assigned across fields in the second and third character positions of the tag to indicate data of the same type. For example, tags reading "X10" contain information about 12.___

   A. topical terms
   B. bibliographic titles
   C. uniform titles
   D. corporate names

13. A librarian wants to subscribe to an e-mail newsletter that contains annotations of information technology articles and other items written by a team of librarians and library staff. She is wary, however, of having her inbox clogged with unread material that arrives too frequently for her to read it all, and would prefer to have the newsletter arrive monthly. The librarian should subscribe to 13.____

A. *Free Pint*
B. *Edupage*
C. *Current Cites*
D. *NewsScan*

14. A journal's "impact factor," a measure of its relative importance, is most often defined as the ______ in a given year. 14.____

A. number of electronic queries coming from a library database
B. frequency of citations to its articles
C. number of top-rated professionals or scholars who publish in it
D. times the full-text is displayed on a library terminal

15. ______ is the online database designed and maintained since 1995 by the Library of Congress to make legislative information accessible to the public 15.____

A. CQ
B. NARA
C. THOMAS
D. FindLaw

16. The main software protocol that manages data on the Internet is 16.____

A. TCP/IP
B. HTTP
C. HTML
D. FTP

17. Which of the following is a repeatable MARC field? 17.____

A. 100
B. 246
C. 250
D. 260

18. A user seeking articles about transportation should be directed to Wilson's ______ Index. 18.____

A. Social Sciences
B. Business Periodicals
C. Applied Science and Technology
D. General Science

19. In the library literature, materials designated with the collecting level "4" in relation to a given subject are considered 19.____

A. "out of scope"
B. sources of basic information
C. comprehensive and authoritative
D. useful for the support of research in the given subject

20. In Web addresses, the hashmark is used to 20.____

A. create a link to another location in the same document
B. identify a port
C. create a link to another Web page
D. differentiate numerical characters

21. The content of a Web site is difficult to navigate, and users tend to get confused when trying to find information. The resource assessment guideline that needs to be addressed is 21.____

A. Documentation and Credibility
B. Ease of Use, Navigation, and Accessibility
C. User Interface and Design
D. Content

22. To extend the accessibility of any material that can be displayed at a library workstation to those with extremely poor vision, _______ can be used. 22.____

A. screen reading software
B. screen magnifying software
C. TTY
D. an on-screen keyboard

23. The software application needed to read files in Portable Document Format (PDF) is known as 23.____

A. Acrobat Reader
B. Real Page
C. Pagemaker
D. techexplorer Hypermedia Browser

24. In data that is prepared in the cataloging-in-publication (CIP) format and distributed in MARC format prior to a work's publication, the element that typically appears after the notes about bibliographical references or previous editions is the 24.____

A. Library of Congress classification number
B. statement of responsibility
C. ISBN
D. Dewey Decimal classification number

25. The reason for the slow pace of initial acceptance of WORM (write once, read many) technology in library archiving is that 25.____

A. the amount of storage available on the disks is too variable to offer predictable capacity
B. disks are not standardized and can be read only on the type of drive used to write them
C. the data cannot be altered once it is stored
D. the longevity of the disk media is still unknown

KEY (CORRECT ANSWERS)

1.	D	6.	A	11.	A	16.	A	21.	B
2.	B	7.	D	12.	D	17.	B	22.	A
3.	D	8.	A	13.	C	18.	C	23.	A
4.	D	9.	C	14.	B	19.	D	24.	C
5.	B	10.	B	15.	C	20.	A	25.	B

TEST 2

DIRECTIONS: Each question or incomplete statement is followed by several suggested answers or completions. Select the one that BEST answers the question or completes the statement. *PRINT THE LETTER OF THE CORRECT ANSWER IN THE SPACE AT THE RIGHT.*

1. Which of the following is NOT an aggregator service? 1.____

   A. ScienceDirect
   B. JSTOR
   C. Britannica
   D. Blackwell's Electronic Journal Navigator

2. Technical service librarians are usually concerned with any of the following, EXCEPT 2.____

   A. repairing damaged materials
   B. checking in journals
   C. cataloging books
   D. checking books out

3. Materials that are published electronically are identified by their 3.____

   A. EAD
   B. DOI
   C. XLS
   D. ISBN

4. Which of the following is an example of "mobile code" that allows a Web designer to incorporate computer programs, such as Flash pages, into Web page content? 4.____

   A. Packet
   B. Worm
   C. Warez
   D. Applet

5. The abbreviation "NOP" on a publisher's invoice usually means the requested item 5.____

   A. is on back order
   B. is not in print
   C. the requested item is not published by the vendor
   D. has not yet been published, but will be in the future

6. A well-designed online catalog or bibliographic database allows the user to employ limiting parameters to restrict the retrieval or entries including the terms included in the search statement. Which of the following is NOT a common example of these "limiters?" 6.____

   A. Spelling
   B. Publication date
   C. Full-text
   D. Locally held

7. Which of the following is LEAST likely to be a guideline followed in setting up an electronic reserves (ER) system in an academic library? 7._____

   A. Restrict access to authorized users off-site, but maintain open access on-site.
   B. Limit offsite access by course and/or instructor name.
   C. Remove or suppress access at the end of every session.
   D. Post copyright warning notices.

8. Subsystems of the Internet include 8._____

   I. the World Wide Web
   II. Newsgroups
   III. Telnet
   IV. e-mail

   A. I only
   B. I, II and III
   C. II and III
   D. I, II, III and IV

9. Binary scanning at 300 dots per inch (dpi) is usually considered adequate for 9._____

   A. halftones
   B. illustrated text
   C. typed or laser-printed archival documents
   D. published text/line art

10. The systems librarian's responsibilities typically include each of the following, EXCEPT 10._____

    A. development and maintenance of hardware and software
    B. Webmaster
    C. training staff in the use of library systems
    D. interlibrary loan processing

11. A records survey is LEAST likely to be used for the purpose of determining the _______ of archival records. 11._____

    A. quality
    B. content
    C. physical quantities
    D. provenance

12. In the searching of an electronic database, which of the following might cause a "false drop?" 12._____

    A. The omission of older information
    B. Too-frequent updating of the database
    C. A word with more than one meaning
    D. Restrictions on database use

13. A group of librarians is meeting to determine the selection of electronic journals for a library's collection. One of the MOST likely disadvantages of including the reference librarian in this group is that he may not 13.___

A. have close contact with users
B. be accustomed to the collaborative approach
C. be able to relinquish his primary responsibilities for long enough periods of time
D. have experience selecting and supporting electronic resources

14. Most Internet service providers (ISPs) are built on ______ lines. 14.___

A. 56 Kbps
B. ISDN
C. T-1
D. T-3

15. Which of the following is a term used to denote a hard copy enlargement of an image on microform? 15.___

A. Blowback
B. Macroform
C. Aperture card
D. Blowup

16. On the Web or in an online bibliography, well-designed search software is capable of 16.___

I. searching more than one database simultaneously
II. removing duplicate record s from results when searching multiple databases
III. viewing search terms highlighted in results
IV. printing, e-mailing, and downloading results in various formats

A. I only
B. I and III
C. III only
D. I, II, III and IV

17. Subject heading systems do NOT 17.___

A. assist searchers in understanding how a specific subject fits into a larger structure of knowledge
B. divide knowledge over 30 broad categories
C. describe what a book or article is about
D. allow people to search by subject area

18. In order to ensure the integrity of digital archive, the origin and chain of custody of a particular file or record most be preserved. This feature of information integrity is known as 18.___

A. content
B. provenance
C. content
D. fixity

19. The creation of a Web page could involve 19.____
    I. using a dedicated Web authoring software program
    II. converting a word-processed document to HTML
    III. converting a magazine article, with images, to PDF
    IV. use the Web authoring capability of a portal

    A. I and II
    B. I, II and IV
    C. II and III
    D. II, III and IV

20. What is the general term for an indexable concept that is assigned to add depth to subject indexing, and that is not listed in the thesaurus of indexing terms because it either represents a proper name or a concept that is not yet authorized for inclusion in the bibliographic database? 20.____

    A. assigner
    B. identifier
    C. descriptor
    D. ideogram

21. The *World of Learning* is an example of a(n) 21.____

    A. concordance
    B. encyclopedia
    C. abstract
    D. directory

22. In the United States, the professional association for academic libraries and librarians is the 22.____

    A. Association of College and Research Libraries (ACRL)
    B. Association of Specialized and Cooperative Library Agencies (ASCLA)
    C. American Library Association (ALA)
    D. National Commission on Libraries and Information Science (NCLIS)

23. The module of the library automation system that is used by the public for interacting with the system is the 23.____

    A. circulation module
    B. serials module
    C. OPAC
    D. cataloging module

24. Which of the following is a synthetic classification system? 24.____

    A. Dewey Decimal
    B. Colon classification
    C. Library of Congress classification
    D. Sears List

25. Library issues concerning the USA Patriot Act include 25.___
    I. civil liberties related to privacy and confidentiality
    II. denial of access to information
    III. fair use
    IV. copyright law

A. I and II
B. II only
C. II, III and IV
D. I, II, III and IV

KEY (CORRECT ANSWERS)

1.	C	6.	A	11.	A	16.	D	21.	D
2.	D	7.	A	12.	C	17.	B	22.	A
3.	B	8.	D	13.	C	18.	B	23.	C
4.	D	9.	C	14.	C	19.	B	24.	B
5.	C	10.	D	15.	A	20.	B	25.	A

EXAMINATION SECTION
TEST 1

DIRECTIONS: Each question or incomplete statement is followed by several suggested answers or completions. Select the one that BEST answers the question or completes the statement. *PRINT THE LETTER OF THE CORRECT ANSWER IN THE SPACE AT THE RIGHT.*

1. The heart of a MARC record for a separately-cataloged electronic journal is contained in the _______ fields 1._____

   A. 0XX
   B. 3XX
   C. 5XX
   D. 7XX

2. Which of the following is NOT an online acquisitions tool? 2._____

   A. *JSTOR*
   B. *Blackwell's Collection Manager*
   C. *Books in Print*
   D. *GOBI*

3. The in-house approach to digital imaging and preservation typically offers each of the following advantages, EXCEPT 3._____

   A. heightened security
   B. learning by doing
   C. quality assurance
   D. predictable per-image costs

4. The publication date of a reference book is usually found on the 4._____

   A. back cover
   B. title page
   C. page immediately before the title page
   D. page immediately following the title page

5. In the Dublin Core Metadata Initiative, an international effort to develop standard mechanisms for searching online resources, the "type" element provides information about the 5._____

   A. topic of the content of the resource, typically expressed as keywords or classification codes
   B. rights held in and over the resource
   C. nature or genre of the content of the resource
   D. extent or scope of the resource's content

6. _______ indexing is a method in which the subject headings or descriptors assigned to document s represent simple concepts that the user must combine at the time of searching to retrieve information on a complex subject. 6._____

   A. String B. Assignment
   C. Pre-coordinate D. Post-coordinate

7. A library server would most likely NOT be used as 7.____

   A. a terminal for searching online resources such as periodical databases
   B. a file server hosting work processing and other office software, along with staff documents and other files
   C. the host computer for the library's automation system
   D. a connection point between the library and the Internet

8. Under copyright law, any rights that eventually revert to the copyright holder when the time period or purpose stated in the contract has elapsed or been discharged are known as _______ rights. 8.____

   A. volume
   B. serial
   C. residual
   D. subsidiary

9. Research indicates that to most library professionals, _______ is the most frequently applied criterion for evaluating the appropriateness of bibliographic references. 9.____

   A. quality
   B. topicality
   C. novelty
   D. availability

10. The best way to minimize the substrate deformation and mistracking of magnetic media is to 10.____

    A. use acetate, rather than polyester
    B. limit playback as much as possible
    C. store the media in constant temperature and humidity
    D. store the media in a room that is warmer and more humid than the rest of the library

11. Which of the following is NOT an advantage associated with purchasing an electronic journal collection in the form of a commercially packaged product? 11.____

    A. Good way to track usage
    B. Searchability of articles from other publishers
    C. Lower price per title
    D. Single search interface

12. In the Dewey Decimal Classification System, works in Natural Sciences and Mathematics are classified in the number category 12.____

    A. 000
    B. 300
    C. 500
    D. 700

13. A library's OPAC allows users to turn off images in Web pages and see only the text during searches. This is an example of interface management called 13.____

A. ghosting
B. graceful degradation
C. funneling
D. cache emptying

14. Which of the following events in library automation occurred FIRST? 14.____

A. The growing importance of "add-ons" related to the delivery of digital content
B. Integration into the Web environment
C. The development of the machine-readable catalog record (MARC)
D. Integration of library systems with learning management systems

15. One of the main advantages associated with searching for information using print indexes is that they 15.____

A. provide cross-references to other topics
B. are usually faster than online searches
C. tend to yield information that is more accurate
D. are usually more current

16. Which of the following statements about online link resolvers is FALSE? 16.____

A. They are applications designed to match source citations with target resources.
B. Most do not store data, but merely establish links.
C. Most accept citation information in the form of an OpenURL.
D. They are designed to take into account which materials a user is authorized by subscription or licensing agreement to access.

17. The intended purpose of copyright law is NOT to 17.____

A. deter others from plagiarizing a work
B. ensure a fair return on an author's or publisher's investment of time and money into the creation of a work
C. provide an author or publisher with the incentive to produce a work by granting a limited monopoly
D. reward innovators at the expense of consumers

18. When using a library's OPAC, a patron moves the mouse to pass a cursor over an image in the Web page and holds the cursor over the image for several seconds. A text message pops up, replacing the information content of the image. This feature, designed for visually impaired users, is enabled by the use of _______ in coding the page. 18.____

A. applets
B. alt tags
C. plug-ins
D. SGML

19. A search of a database containing 100 records relevant to a topic retrieves 50 records, 25 of which are relevant to the topic. The search is said to have a ______ percent recall. 19.____

A. 10
B. 25
C. 50
D. 75

20. In a bibliography compiled in the MLA format, the authorship of a book by Tom and Bridget Jones would be indicated 20.____

A. Jones, Tom and Bridget Jones
B. Jones, Tom and Bridget
C. Jones, Tom and Jones, Bridget
D. Tom Jones and Bridget Jones

21. In most large libraries, the ______ record is attached to the bibliographic record for a serial title or multivolume item to track issues, parts, or volumes as they are acquired by the library. 21.____

A. item
B. check-in
C. order
D. holdings

22. Which of the following is an online bibliographic database vendor that charges on a per-search basis? 22.____

A. EBSCO
B. FirstSearch
C. ProQuest
D. Gale Group

23. What is the term for the blending of current and emerging technologies into a single multi-use device? 23.____

A. Virtual reality
B. Convergence
C. Processing
D. Artificial intelligence

24. Which of the following is an approach to interoperability that uses proxies as interfaces between existing systems? 24.____

A. HotJava
B. TeX
C. InfoBus
D. STARTS

25. The Metadata Object Description Schema, or MODS, 25.____
    I. is an XML schema
    II. was created by the Library of Congress for representing MARC-like semantics
    III. can be used to carry selected data from MARC21 records
    IV. cannot be used for the conversion of MARC to XML without loss of data

    A. I and II
    B. I, II and IV
    C. II and III
    D. I, II, III and IV

KEY (CORRECT ANSWERS)

1. C
2. A
3. D
4. D
5. C
6. D
7. A
8. C
9. B
10. C
11. B
12. C
13. B
14. C
15. A
16. B
17. D
18. B
19. B
20. A
21. D
22. B
23. B
24. C
25. D

TEST 2

DIRECTIONS: Each question or incomplete statement is followed by several suggested answers or completions. Select the one that BEST answers the question or completes the statement. *PRINT THE LETTER OF THE CORRECT ANSWER IN THE SPACE AT THE RIGHT.*

1. The main advantage to using an intermediary service for access to electronic journals is that 1.___

   A. one search engine will search the contents of journals from several publishers and/or disciplines
   B. the one-time start-up cost is predictable
   C. the databases will have citations and abstracts only for articles that are available in full-text
   D. the depth of backfiles is predictable

2. A library automation system needs to be able to search compatible resources from a single interface, and to search text files based on keywords. 2.___
   The standard query language that is used for this is

   A. WAIS
   B. Gopher
   C. ODBC
   D. Z39.50

3. Under copyright law, the rights to publish a work in a form other than the original publication–for example, in installments in a periodical–are known as ______ rights. 3.___

   A. residual
   B. subsidiary
   C. site-specific
   D. residual

4. ______ indexing is a method in which multiple concepts are combined by the indexer to form subject headings or descriptors assigned to documents dealing with complex subjects. 4.___

   A. Derivative
   B. Pre-coordinate
   C. String
   D. Post-coordinate

5. Which of the following terms is associated with efforts to bridge the digital divide? 5.___

   A. E-rate
   B. Intellectual property
   C. Artificial intelligence
   D. Convergence

6. After deciding to offer users online access to an electronic journals collection through the library's online catalog, a library must decide whether to use the "single-record" or "separate-record" approach to offering access to print and electronic versions. Advantages of the separate-record approach include the fact that it is 6.____

   I. better suited to handle linking relationships between formats
   II. it is prescribed by AACR2 (Anglo-American Cataloging Rules)
   III. used by the Government Printing Office (GPO)
   IV. preferred by the Cooperative Online Serials Program (CONSER)

   A. I only
   B. II and III
   C. I, II and IV
   D. I, II, III and IV

7. One of the key issues in remote access to library automated systems today is 7.____

   A. authentication
   B. free speech
   C. cost
   D. training

8. Which of the following is NOT a multiple-access database? 8.____

   A. A printed dictionary arranged alphabetically by headword
   B. A library catalog searchable by author, title, subject, and keywords
   C. A bibliographic database searchable by author, title, subject, or date
   D. A printed encyclopedia in alphabetical sections, with a subject or keyword index to the entire work at the end of the last volume.

9. Which of the following services is LEAST likely to be offered by a jobber? 9.____

   A. Approval plans
   B. Continuation orders
   C. Technical processing
   D. Online searchable bibliographies

10. Modern (5th generation) computers are most specifically characterized by the feature of 10.____

    A. transistors
    B. integrated chips
    C. multiprocessing
    D. data communications

11. In library acquisitions, a purchase order becomes a contract when 11.____

    A. the seller receives the invoice
    B. it is accepted by the purchaser
    C. the purchaser signs the invoice
    D. it is accepted by the seller

12. The primary metadata that describes a social science data set is a 12.____

    A. codebook
    B. unicode
    C. chapbook
    D. METS

13. The contents of a single CD-ROM are roughly equivalent to the contents of about ______ books. 13.___

A. 15
B. 120
C. 300
D. 250

14. Which of the following is NOT a link resolver? 14.___

A. ICate
B. PURL
C. SFX
D. Linkfinder Plus

15. Historical works are classified in the Library of Congress Classification System under the broad category designated 15.___

A. L
B. H
C. D
D. S

16. The most widely used medium for offline data storage is 16.___

A. CD-ROM
B. RAID
C. DVD-ROM
D. magnetic tape

17. In archives, the legal term for a record or document that is no longer in the possession of its original creator or legitimate custodian is 17.___

A. dangler
B. estray
C. abductee
D. orphan

18. The largest unit in a database is a 18.___

A. file
B. record
C. subfield
D. field

19. Which of the following is NOT typically part of an item record? 19.___

A. Price
B. Volume number
C. Vendor
D. Barcode

20. Which of the following is an advantage associated with the "scan-first" approach to preservation-in which microfilm records are produced from digitized scans of original documents? 20.____

    A. Wide range of equipment and service vendors
    B. Unsettled standards for preservation
    C. Adjustments can be made prior to conversion
    D. Higher image resolution than analog photography

21. Communications from an author to the editor of a journal typically do NOT include 21.____

    A. proof of permission
    B. referee comments
    C. article appropriate query
    D. copyright assignment

22. Which of the following is NOT a primary source? 22.____

    A. Memoir/autobiography
    B. Encyclopedia
    C. Minutes from an organization or agency
    D. Speech

23. A user initiates an online search by typing "author = Shakespeare." This is an example of a ______ search. 23.____

    A. fielded
    B. Boolean
    C. full-text
    D. stop-list

24. Asyndetic references or bibliographies 24.____

    A. lack descriptors
    B. include embedded hypertext
    C. focus on semantic relationships between topics
    D. lack cross-references

25. The most universally accepted criteria for weeding library items are based on 25.____

    A. subject area
    B. date of publication
    C. the condition or physical description of the item
    D. content

KEY (CORRECT ANSWERS)

1. A
2. D
3. B
4. B
5. A

6. C
7. A
8. A
9. D
10. C

11. D
12. A
13. C
14. B
15. C

16. D
17. B
18. A
19. C
20. C

21. B
22. B
23. A
24. D
25. C

EXAMINATION SECTION
TEST 1

DIRECTIONS: Each question or incomplete statement is followed by several suggested answers or completions. Select the one that BEST answers the question or completes the statement. *PRINT THE LETTER OF THE CORRECT ANSWER IN THE SPACE AT THE RIGHT.*

1. The BEST known encyclopedia in the Western world, first published in the 18th century, was 1.____

   A. WORLD BOOK ENCYCLOPEDIA
   B. COMPTON'S PICTURED ENCYCLOPEDIA
   C. ENCYCLOPEDIA BRITANNICA
   D. ENCYCLOPEDIA AMERICANA

2. Authority-control records are important in an online catalog environment because they 2.____

   A. help prevent *blind* cross-references
   B. expand the capacity of the database
   C. keep the system from overloading
   D. provide access to fugitive materials

3. Which of the following is NOT the name of an online catalog? 3.____

   A. Geobase B. Dynix C. Geac D. OCLC

4. Nom de plume is synonymous with 4.____

   A. pseudonym B. nickname
   C. given name D. telonism

5. Component-word searching is another way of saying ______ searching. 5.____

   A. key-word B. permuterm
   C. subject D. author/title

6. The citation indexes (SCIENCE CITATION INDEX, etc.) are unique in that they 6.____

   A. allow searching by the name of an institution
   B. provide access to foreign language journals
   C. allow searching of an author's references
   D. contain millions of unique records

7. A good online public access catalog (OPAC) can be expected to provide all of the following EXCEPT 7.____

   A. author and title access to books and audio-visual materials
   B. the loan status of materials that circulate
   C. information regarding who a book has been loaned to
   D. the place and publisher of each book in the catalog

8. Of the points to consider in a systematic evaluation of an encyclopedia, the LEAST important one is 8.____

   A. cost B. viewpoint and objectivity
   C. subject coverage D. number of pages

9. Widespread searching of bibliographic databases dates back to 9.____

A. the 1950's
B. 1960
C. the mid-1980's
D. the early 1970's

10. The format of a reference set means the 10.____

A. writing style
B. binding and size
C. authority of contributors
D. viewpoint and objectivity

11. The FIRST bibliographic databases were by-products of 11.____

A. progress in NASA technology
B. online card catalogs such as OCLC
C. information dissemination centers
D. the computerized typesetting operation

12. A patron asks your advice as a librarian on a set of encyclopedias he is considering for his family. 12.____
The MOST helpful response for you is to

A. give limited advice and provide the patron with professional reviews of the set under question
B. give no advice for fear of repercussions from sales-persons and publishers
C. endorse or condemn the set whole-heartedly, depending on your own opinion
D. refer the patron to the director of the library

13. The four basic components of the online industry include all of the following EXCEPT 13.____

A. libraries and information centers
B. library school administrators
C. end-users who request information
D. database producers

14. McGraw-Hill's ENCYCLOPEDIA OF WORLD ART is an example of a ______ encyclopedia. 14.____

A. children's
B. subject
C. supermarket
D. foreign

15. Which of the following bibliographic databases is NOT produced by a federal government agency or federally-supported institution? 15.____

A. ERIC
B. COMPENDEX
C. AGRICOLA
D. MEDLINE

16. A ready-reference work is one which 16.____

A. is allowed to circulate outside of the library
B. is especially difficult to use
C. arrives on a monthly basis
D. is useful for *quick* questions of a factual nature

17. All of the following are examples of source documents EXCEPT 17.____

A. patents
B. conference papers
C. indexes
D. newspapers

18. The STATISTICAL ABSTRACT OF THE UNITED STATES is a compendium in the sense that it 18.____

A. contains statistics on a wide range of subjects
B. is published on an annual basis
C. is a summary of U.S. Census data
D. can be used for research in education

19. The number EJ121478, as part of an ERIC record, would indicate that the material referenced 19.____

A. is a journal article
B. is a book
C. is an ERIC document on microfiche
D. was entered in the database in 1978

20. A thesaurus which accompanies an index such as ERIC is a list of 20.____

A. corporate authors
B. journals indexed
C. stop words
D. assigned descriptors

KEY (CORRECT ANSWERS)

1.	C	11.	D
2.	A	12.	A
3.	A	13.	B
4.	A	14.	B
5.	A	15.	B
6.	C	16.	D
7.	C	17.	C
8.	D	18.	C
9.	D	19.	A
10.	B	20.	D

TEST 2

DIRECTIONS: Each question or incomplete statement is followed by several suggested answers or completions. Select the one that BEST answers the question or completes the statement. *PRINT THE LETTER OF THE CORRECT ANSWER IN THE SPACE AT THE RIGHT.*

1. The U.S. National Library of Medicine produces all of the following databases EXCEPT 1.____

   A. EMBASE B. AIDSLINE C. CANCERLIT D. MEDLINE

2. H.W. Wilson's CURRENT BIOGRAPHY provides 2.____

   A. essay-length biographical information
   B. reference to information in BIOGRAPHY INDEX
   C. no more information on an individual than is provided by WHO'S WHO
   D. reviews of best-selling biographies

3. The database which provides access to fugitive materials in education is 3.____

   A. Academic Index
   B. Education Index
   C. ERIC
   D. Mental Measurements Yearbook

4. All of the following are covered in CONTEMPORARY AUTHORS EXCEPT 4.____

   A. screenwriters
   B. poets
   C. dramatists
   D. technical writers

5. Boolean logic utilizes all of the following logical operators EXCEPT 5.____

   A. if B. or C. not D. and

6. A prescriptive dictionary is one which 6.____

   A. discusses in great detail the origin of a word
   B. adheres to tradition and historical authority for word definitions and approved usage
   C. attempts to relate every possible definition and usage of a word
   D. is published only in the United States

7. Free-text searching in a bibliographic database means 7.____

   A. searching several descriptors at one time
   B. using Boolean logic in your search
   C. searching without the use of controlled vocabulary
   D. searching only titles and abstracts

8. ABRIDGED INDEX MEDICUS differs from INDEX MEDICUS in that it 8.____

   A. contains citations to English-language journals only
   B. contains only information from the last twelve months
   C. contains citations to foreign-language journals only
   D. is not published by the National Library of Medicine

17. All of the following are examples of source documents EXCEPT 17.____

A. patents
B. conference papers
C. indexes
D. newspapers

18. The STATISTICAL ABSTRACT OF THE UNITED STATES is a compendium in the sense that it 18.____

A. contains statistics on a wide range of subjects
B. is published on an annual basis
C. is a summary of U.S. Census data
D. can be used for research in education

19. The number EJ121478, as part of an ERIC record, would indicate that the material referenced 19.____

A. is a journal article
B. is a book
C. is an ERIC document on microfiche
D. was entered in the database in 1978

20. A thesaurus which accompanies an index such as ERIC is a list of 20.____

A. corporate authors
B. journals indexed
C. stop words
D. assigned descriptors

KEY (CORRECT ANSWERS)

1. C
2. A
3. A
4. A
5. A
6. C
7. C
8. D
9. D
10. B
11. D
12. A
13. B
14. B
15. B
16. D
17. C
18. C
19. A
20. D

TEST 2

DIRECTIONS: Each question or incomplete statement is followed by several suggested answers or completions. Select the one that BEST answers the question or completes the statement. *PRINT THE LETTER OF THE CORRECT ANSWER IN THE SPACE AT THE RIGHT.*

1. The U.S. National Library of Medicine produces all of the following databases EXCEPT 1.____

   A. EMBASE B. AIDSLINE C. CANCERLIT D. MEDLINE

2. H.W. Wilson's CURRENT BIOGRAPHY provides 2.____

   A. essay-length biographical information
   B. reference to information in BIOGRAPHY INDEX
   C. no more information on an individual than is provided by WHO'S WHO
   D. reviews of best-selling biographies

3. The database which provides access to fugitive materials in education is 3.____

   A. Academic Index
   B. Education Index
   C. ERIC
   D. Mental Measurements Yearbook

4. All of the following are covered in CONTEMPORARY AUTHORS EXCEPT 4.____

   A. screenwriters
   B. poets
   C. dramatists
   D. technical writers

5. Boolean logic utilizes all of the following logical operators EXCEPT 5.____

   A. if B. or C. not D. and

6. A prescriptive dictionary is one which 6.____

   A. discusses in great detail the origin of a word
   B. adheres to tradition and historical authority for word definitions and approved usage
   C. attempts to relate every possible definition and usage of a word
   D. is published only in the United States

7. Free-text searching in a bibliographic database means 7.____

   A. searching several descriptors at one time
   B. using Boolean logic in your search
   C. searching without the use of controlled vocabulary
   D. searching only titles and abstracts

8. ABRIDGED INDEX MEDICUS differs from INDEX MEDICUS in that it 8.____

   A. contains citations to English-language journals only
   B. contains only information from the last twelve months
   C. contains citations to foreign-language journals only
   D. is not published by the National Library of Medicine

9. The two PRINCIPAL operations of public services are 9.____

A. circulation and reference
B. reference and serials management
C. circulation and collection development
D. reference and classification

10. Of the following reasons for an academic library to acquire the DICTIONARY OF AMERICAN SLANG, which is the LEAST valid? 10.____

A. Most regular dictionaries do not indicate the variations of meaning of given slang terms or words.
B. Students often come across expressions which are not defined well in ordinary dictionaries.
C. It is a good source to check on the language used by an author to convey a character's background or social class.
D. Students and librarians alike enjoy reading through it during their leisure time.

11. Collection maintenance includes all of the following EXCEPT 11.____

A. taking inventory
B. reshelving books
C. identifying overdues
D. shelf-reading

12. A gazetteer is a 12.____

A. biographical dictionary
B. good source for looking up phases of the moon
C. geographical dictionary
D. guide to motels throughout the United States

13. A Dewey Decimal Classification number never has MORE than how many digits to the LEFT of the decimal? 13.____

A. Four
B. Five
C. Three
D. Two

14. In MOST government depository libraries, the government documents are arranged on the shelves 14.____

A. by Superintendent of Documents numbers
B. by Library of Congress call numbers
C. by Dewey Decimal numbers
D. alphabetically by title

15. The Library of Congress Classification System is different from the Dewey Decimal Classification System in that it 15.____

A. arranges books on the shelf by subject
B. does not include author numbers
C. is not frequently used by libraries in the United States
D. was developed to meet the needs of a specific library's collection

16. The BEST reference source for finding, in detail, the organization and activities of all U.S. government agencies is 16.____

    A. POLITICS IN AMERICA
    B. THE STATESMAN'S YEARBOOK
    C. UNITED STATES GOVERNMENT MANUAL
    D. MOODY'S MUNICIPAL AND GOVERNMENT MANUAL

17. The added entries in a catalog record could be for 17.____

    A. joint authors, titles, or series
    B. joint authors, series, or subjects
    C. joint authors, titles, or subjects
    D. titles, publishers, or series

18. Which of the following illustrates a directional question? 18.____

    A. How far is Syracuse from Lake Ontario?
    B. Where is the public telephone?
    C. Where can I find a biographical dictionary of presidents?
    D. Is Italy to the east of Spain?

19. You are performing an online bibliographic search for a patron and have brought up a set consisting of 300 records. 19.____
    Of the following, which is the LEAST valid way of limiting the search in order to avoid printing such a large set?

    A. Limit the search to a certain range of years
    B. Redefine the search using more specific descriptors
    C. Print only the first 40 records of the set
    D. Cut out references to articles in languages the patron cannot read

20. All of the following are examples of primary sources EXCEPT 20.____

    A. diaries
    B. biographies
    C. letters
    D. memoirs

21. *What is the population of Mexico City?* would MOST likely be classified as what type of reference question? 21.____

    A. Ready reference
    B. Directional
    C. Research on a topic
    D. Instructional

22. Something you would NOT expect to find in a vertical file is 22.____

    A. a monograph
    B. a pamphlet
    C. a folded map
    D. newspaper clippings

23. Logical product, logical sum, and logical difference are all part of what type of searching? 23.____

    A. Permuterm logic
    B. Keyword-in-context (KWIC)
    C. Statistical logic
    D. Boolean logic

24. Keyword-in-context (KWIC) indexing is also called ______ indexing. 24.____

    A. title
    B. comprehensive
    C. subject
    D. permutation

25. The MARC format was developed at the 25.____

A. National Library of Medicine
B. British Library
C. Library of Congress
D. Smithsonian Institute

26. Patrons of a general library are usually MOST aware of which of the following library activities? 26.____

A. Circulation
B. Accession
C. Cataloging
D. Reference

27. Three of the following four are consequences of the copyrighting of books by the U.S. government. 27.____
Which is NOT such a consequence?

A. Protecting author's rights
B. Encouraging writing
C. Securing deposit material for the government
D. Government endorsement of the copyrighted texts

28. The term *cataloging in publication* refers to a cataloging program under which cataloging information 28.____

A. appears in the PUBLISHERS' WEEKLY
B. appears in the National Union Catalog
C. appears in the publication itself
D. is prepared by the publisher

29. The MAJOR use of a formal statement of a library's objective is 29.____

A. serving as a guideline for program development and services
B. justifying library staffing to the board and public
C. convincing the governing body of the need for financial support
D. training library staff in improved methods and practices

30. Circulation statistics should be gathered PRIMARILY for the purpose of 30.____

A. justifying the library budget
B. improving library service
C. cutting library costs
D. analyzing personnel performance

KEY (CORRECT ANSWERS)

1.	A	16.	C
2.	A	17.	A
3.	C	18.	B
4.	D	19.	C
5.	A	20.	B
6.	B	21.	A
7.	C	22.	A
8.	A	23.	D
9.	A	24.	D
10.	D	25.	C
11.	C	26.	A
12.	C	27.	D
13.	C	28.	C
14.	A	29.	A
15.	D	30.	B

TEST 3

DIRECTIONS: Each question or incomplete statement is followed by several suggested answers or completions. Select the one that BEST answers the question or completes the statement. *PRINT THE LETTER OF THE CORRECT ANSWER IN THE SPACE AT THE RIGHT.*

1. A typical reference in the READER'S GUIDE TO PERIODICAL LITERATURE would include all of the following EXCEPT 1.____

   A. author
   B. title of the article
   C. journal name
   D. journal abstract

2. An example of a subject authority list used in cataloging is the 2.____

   A. THESAURUS OF ERIC DESCRIPTORS
   B. LIBRARY OF CONGRESS SUBJECT HEADINGS
   C. NEW YORK TIMES INDEX
   D. CINAHL SUBJECT HEADING LIST

3. An example of a nonperiodical serial is 3.____

   A. EUROPA YEARBOOK
   B. AQUACULTURE MAGAZINE
   C. THE WASHINGTON POST
   D. JOURNAL OF THE AMERICAN MEDICAL ASSOCIATION

4. The Superintendent of Documents classification system arranges government documents on the shelves 4.____

   A. alphabetically by title
   B. by government agency
   C. alphabetically by author
   D. according to date of printing

5. Which of the following is an example of an open-ended question? 5.____

   A. Would you like books or magazine articles?
   B. You say you need to know the elevation of Denver?
   C. What kind of information about sharks are you looking for?
   D. Have you ever used our online catalog?

6. Scientific Information's weekly CURRENT CONTENTS consists of 6.____

   A. reproductions of journal contents pages
   B. a subject index for scientific journals
   C. author and title indexes for current periodicals
   D. scientific journal abstracts

7. All of the following are bibliographic utilities involved in resource sharing EXCEPT 7.____

   A. OCLC
   B. RLIN
   C. DYNIX
   D. UTLAS

8. The MAIN objective of reference negotiation is to 8.____

A. save the librarian's time
B. steer patrons away from heavily used sources
C. find out what the patron specifically needs
D. instruct patrons in the proper use of reference materials

9. Which of the following PROPERLY demonstrates a logical product and logical difference search statement? 9.____

A. Dogs and cats, not birds
B. (Dogs or cats) and not birds
C. Dogs and not birds or cats
D. Dogs and (cats or birds)

10. The generally accepted definition of a serial includes all of the following EXCEPT 10.____

A. yearbooks
B. newspapers
C. theses
D. journals

11. ESSAY AND GENERAL LITERATURE INDEX is MOST useful for locating 11.____

A. a specific chapter of a book
B. magazine and journal articles
C. biographical essays
D. a pamphlet or newsletter

12. What do LIBRARY JOURNAL, SHEEHY'S GUIDE TO REFERENCE BOOKS, and ARBA have in common? 12.____
They

A. are all periodicals
B. discuss management of online catalogs
C. provide critical evaluation of reference materials
D. discuss only highly recommended reference sources

13. SHORT STORY INDEX covers stories published 13.____

A. on all subjects except science fiction
B. in collections and the NEW YORK TIMES
C. in collections and periodicals
D. by American authors only

14. One way in which nonperiodical serials (such as yearbooks) are different from periodical serials (such as journals) is that nonperiodicals are 14.____

A. published several times a year
B. usually a collection of articles
C. usually ordered by subscription
D. usually acquired through a standing order

15. Of the general serial sources listed below, which is the only one that includes newspapers? 15.____

    A. STANDARD PERIODICAL DIRECTORY
    B. GALE DIRECTORY OF PUBLICATIONS
    C. ULRICH'S INTERNATIONAL PERIODICALS DIRECTORY
    D. IRREGULAR SERIALS AND ANNUALS

16. The READER'S GUIDE TO PERIODICAL LITERATURE indexes 16.____

    A. magazines and newspapers
    B. popular magazines
    C. scholarly journals
    D. short story anthologies

17. Ethnic numbers are added to classification symbols so as to arrange books by 17.____

    A. subject
    B. place of printing
    C. author
    D. language

18. End-matter items could include all of the following EXCEPT 18.____

    A. appendices
    B. bibliographies
    C. tables of contents
    D. indexes

19. Which of the following BEST describes a jobber? 19.____
    A

    A. company which produces databases
    B. corporate body responsible for placing a book on the market
    C. wholesale bookseller who stocks books and supplies them to libraries
    D. person skilled in writing computer programs

20. The word *an* is a stopword on the Medline database. 20.____
    This means that

    A. it cannot be used as a search term in the database
    B. Medline includes articles such as *an* and *the* when alphabetizing by title
    C. if you type in that word, you will exit the database
    D. you cannot use Medline when searching for a title that begins with *an*

21. Of the following queries, which could NOT be answered by consulting a regular dictionary? 21.____

    A. What is the Golden Rule?
    B. How deep is a fathom?
    C. Does "humble" come from the same root as "human"?
    D. What are the rules for writing a sonnet?

22. An accurate definition of annals would be a(n) 22.____

    A. serial publication issued once a year
    B. anonymous publication
    C. record of events arranged in chronological order
    D. bibliography of an author's writings arranged by date of publication

23. West's FEDERAL PRACTICE DIGEST is an index to 23.____

    A. United States Supreme Court cases
    B. United States statutes
    C. New York State statutes
    D. The Code of Federal Regulations

24. MOST federal government documents are printed by 24.____

    A. the Government Printing Office
    B. the Library of Congress
    C. the United States Printing Office
    D. Congress

25. Setting aside a separate section for oversized books is an example of 25.____

    A. subject cataloging
    B. parallel arrangement
    C. a special materials collection
    D. Dewey Decimal Classification

KEY (CORRECT ANSWERS)

1. D
2. B
3. A
4. B
5. C
6. A
7. C
8. C
9. A
10. C
11. A
12. C
13. C
14. D
15. B
16. B
17. D
18. C
19. C
20. A
21. D
22. C
23. A
24. A
25. B

EXAMINATION SECTION
TEST 1

DIRECTIONS: Each question or incomplete statement is followed by several suggested answers or completions. Select the one that BEST answers the question or completes the statement. *PRINT THE LETTER OF THE CORRECT ANSWER IN THE SPACE AT THE RIGHT.*

1. Records of one type or another are kept in every office. The MOST important of the following reasons for the supervisor of a clerical or stenographic unit to keep statistical records of the work done in his unit is generally to 1.____

   A. supply basic information needed in planning the work of the unit
   B. obtain statistics for comparison with other units
   C. serve as the basis for unsatisfactory employee evaluation
   D. provide the basis for special research projects on program budgeting

2. It is better for an employee to report and be responsible directly to several supervisors than to report and be responsible to only one supervisor. 2.____
   This statement directly CONTRADICTS the supervisory principle generally known as

   A. span of control
   B. unity of command
   C. delegation of authority
   D. accountability

3. The one of the following which would MOST likely lead to friction among clerks in a unit is for the unit supervisor to 3.____

   A. defend the actions of his clerks when discussing them with his own supervisor
   B. praise each of his clerks "in confidence" as the best clerk in the unit
   C. get his men to work together as a team in completing the work of the unit
   D. consider the point of view of the rank and file clerks when assigning unpleasant tasks

4. You become aware that one of the employees you supervise has failed to follow correct procedure and has been permitting various reports to be prepared, typed, and transmitted improperly. 4.____
   The BEST action for you to take FIRST in this situation is to

   A. order the employee to review all departmental procedures and reprimand him for having violated them
   B. warn the employee that he must obey regulations because uniformity is essential for effective departmental operation
   C. confer with the employee both about his failure to follow regulations and his reasons for doing so
   D. watch the employee's work very closely in the future but say nothing about this violation

5. The supervisory clerk who would be MOST likely to have poor control over his subordinates is the one who 5.____

   A. goes to unusually great lengths to try to win their approval
   B. pitches in with the work they are doing during periods of heavy workload when no extra help can be obtained

C. encourages and helps his subordinates toward advancement
D. considers suggestions from his subordinates before establishing new work procedures involving them

6. Suppose that a clerk who has been transferred to your office from another division in your agency because of difficulties with his supervisor has been placed under your supervision. 6.____
The BEST course of action for you to take FIRST is to

A. instruct the clerk in the duties he will be performing in your office and make him feel "wanted" in his new position
B. analyze the clerk's past grievance to determine if the transfer was the best solution to the problem
C. advise him of the difficulties that his former supervisor had with other employees and encourage him not to feel badly about the transfer
D. warn him that you will not tolerate any nonsense and that he will be under continuous surveillance while assigned to you

7. A certain office supervisor takes the initiative to represent his employees' interests related to working conditions, opportunities for advancement, etc. to his own supervisor and the administrative levels of the agency. This supervisor's actions will MOST probably have the effect of 7.____

A. preventing employees from developing individual initiative in their work goals
B. encouraging employees to compete openly for the special attention of their supervisor
C. depriving employees of the opportunity to be represented by persons and/or unions of their own choosing
D. building employee confidence in their supervisor and a spirit of cooperation in their work

8. Suppose that you have been promoted, assigned as a supervisor of a certain unit and asked to reorganize its functions so that specific routine procedures can be established. Before deciding which routines to establish, the FIRST of the following steps you should take is to 8.____

A. decide who will perform each task in the routine
B. determine the purpose to be served by each routine procedure
C. outline the sequence of steps in each routine to be established
D. calculate if more staff will be needed to carry out the new procedures

9. When routine procedures covering the ordinary work of an office are established, the supervisor of the office tends to be relieved of the need to 9.____

A. make repeated decisions on the handling of recurring similar situations
B. check the accuracy of the work completed by his subordinates
C. train his subordinates in new work procedures
D. plan and schedule the work of his office

10. Of the following, the method which would be LEAST helpful to a supervisor in effectively applying the principles of on-the-job safety to the daily work of his unit is for him to 10.____

A. initiate corrections of unsafe layouts of equipment and unsafe work processes
B. take charge of operations that are not routine to make certain that safety precautions are established and observed
C. continue to "talk safety" and promote safety consciousness in his subordinates
D. figure the cost of all accidents which could possibly occur on the job

11. A clerk is assigned to serve as receptionist for a large and busy office. Although many members of the public visit this office, the clerk often experiences periods of time in which he has nothing to do. 11.____
In these circumstances, the MOST advisable of the following actions for the supervisor to take is to

A. assign a number of relatively low priority clerical jobs to the receptionist to do in the slow periods
B. regularly rotate this assignment so that all the clerks experience this lighter work load
C. assign the receptionist job as part of the duties of a number of clerks whose desks are nearest the reception room
D. overlook the situation, since most of the receptionist's time is spent in performing a necessary and meaningful function

12. For a supervisor to require all stenographers in a stenographic pool to produce the same amount of work on a particular day is 12.____

A. *advisable;* since it will prove that the supervisor plays no favorites
B. *fair;* since all the stenographers are receiving approximately the same salary, their output should be equivalent
C. *not necessary;* since the fast workers will compensate for the slow workers
D. *not realistic;* since individual differences in abilities and work assignment must be taken into consideration

13. The establishment of a centralized typing pool to service the various units in an organization is MOST likely to be worthwhile when there is 13.____

A. wide fluctuation from time to time in the needs of the various units for typing service
B. a large volume of typing work to be done in each of the units
C. a need by each unit for different kinds of typing service
D. a training program in operation to develop and maintain typing skills

14. A newly appointed supervisor should learn as much as possible about the backgrounds of his subordinates. This statement is generally CORRECT because 14.____

A. knowing their backgrounds assures they will be treated objectively, equally, and without favor
B. effective handling of subordinates is based upon knowledge of their individual differences
C. subordinates perform more efficiently under one supervisor than under another
D. subordinates have confidence in a supervisor who knows all about them

15. The use of electronic computers in modern businesses has produced many changes in office and information management. Of the following, it would NOT be correct to state that computer utilization 15.____

A. broadens the scope of managerial and supervisory authority
B. establishes uniformity in the processing and reporting of information
C. cuts costs by reducing the personnel needed for efficient office operation
D. supplies management rapidly with up-to-date data to facilitate decision-making

16. The CHIEF advantage of having a single, large open office instead of small partitioned ones for a clerical unit or stenographic pool is that the single, large open office 16.____

A. affords privacy without isolation for all office workers not directly dealing with the public
B. assures the smoother, more continuous inter-office flow of work that is essential for efficient work production
C. facilitates the office supervisor's visual control over and communication with his subordinates
D. permits a more decorative and functional arrangement of office furniture and machines

17. When a supervisor provides a new employee with the information necessary for a basic knowledge and a general understanding of practices and procedures of the agency, he is applying the type of training generally known as ______ training. 17.____

A. pre-employment
B. induction
C. on-the-job
D. supervisory

18. Many government agencies require the approval by a central forms control unit of the design and reproduction of new office forms.
The one of the following results of this procedure that is a DISADVANTAGE is that requiring prior approval of a central forms control unit USUALLY 18.____

A. limits the distribution of forms to those offices with justifiable reasons for receiving them
B. permits checking whether existing forms or modifications of them are in line with current agency needs
C. encourages reliance on only the central office to set up all additional forms when needed
D. provides for someone with a specialized knowledge of forms design to review and criticize new and revised forms

19. Suppose that a large quantity of information is in the files which are located a good distance from your desk. Almost every worker in your office must use these files constantly. Your duties in particular require that you daily refer to about 25 of the same items. They are short, one-page items distributed throughout the files.
In this situation, your BEST course would be to 19.____

A. take the items that you use daily from the files and keep them on your desk, inserting "out cards" in their place
B. go to the files each time you need the information so that the items will be there when other workers need them
C. make xerox copies of the information you use most frequently and keep them in your desk for ready reference
D. label the items you use most often with different colored tabs for immediate identification

20. Of the following, the MOST important advantage of preparing manuals of office procedures in loose-leaf form is that this form 20.____

A. permits several employees to use different sections simultaneously
B. facilitates the addition of new material and the removal of obsolete material
C. is more readily arranged in alphabetical order
D. reduces the need for cross-references to locate material carried under several headings

21. Suppose that you establish a new clerical procedure for the unit you supervise. 21.____
Your keeping a close check on the time required by your staff to handle the new procedure is wise MAINLY because such a check will find out

A. whether your subordinates know how to handle the new procedure
B. whether a revision of the unit's work schedule will be necessary as a result of the new procedure
C. what attitude your employees have toward the new procedure
D. what alterations in job descriptions will be necessitated by the new procedure

22. From the viewpoint of an office supervisor, the BEST of the following reasons for distributing the incoming mail *before* the beginning of the regular work day is that 22.____

A. distribution can be handled quickly and most efficiently at that time
B. distribution later in the day may be distracting to or interfere with other employees
C. the employees who distribute the mail can then perform other tasks during the rest of the day
D. office activities for the day based on the mail may then be started promptly

23. Suppose you are the head of a unit with ten staff members who are located in several different rooms. If you want to inform your staff of a *minor* change in procedure, the BEST and LEAST expensive way of doing so would usually be to 23.____

A. send a mimeographed copy to each staff member
B. call a special staff meeting and announce the change
C. circulate a memo, having each staff member initial it
D. have a clerk tell each member of the staff about the change

24. The numbered statements below relate to the stenographic skill of taking dictation. 24.____
According to authorities on secretarial practices, which of these are GENERALLY recommended guides to development of efficient stenographic skills?
A stenographer should

I. date her notebook daily to facilitate locating certain notes at a later time
II. make corrections of grammatical mistakes while her boss is dictating to her
III. draw a line through the dictated matter in her notebook after she has transcribed it
IV. write in longhand unfamiliar names and addresses dictated to her

The CORRECT answer is:

A. I, II, III
B. II, III, IV
C. I, III, IV
D. All of the above

25. A bureau of a city agency is about to move to a new location. 25.____
Of the following, the FIRST step that should be taken in order to provide a good layout for the office at the new location is to

A. decide the exact amount of space to be assigned to each unit of the bureau
B. decide whether to lay out a single large open office or one consisting of small partitioned units
C. ask each unit chief in the bureau to examine the new location and submit a request for the amount of space he needs
D. prepare a detailed plan of the dimensions of the floor space to be occupied by the bureau at the new location

---

KEY (CORRECT ANSWERS)

1. A
2. B
3. B
4. C
5. A
6. A
7. D
8. B
9. A
10. D
11. A
12. D
13. A
14. B
15. A
16. C
17. B
18. C
19. C
20. B
21. B
22. D
23. C
24. C
25. D

TEST 2

DIRECTIONS: Each question or incomplete statement is followed by several suggested answers or completions. Select the one that BEST answers the question or completes the statement. *PRINT THE LETTER OF THE CORRECT ANSWER IN THE SPACE AT THE RIGHT.*

1. Suppose you are the supervisor of the mailroom of a large agency where the mail received daily is opened by machine, sorted by hand for delivery and time-stamped. Letters and any enclosures are removed from envelopes and stapled together before distribution. One of your newest clerks asks you what should be done when a letter makes reference to an enclosure, but no enclosure is in the envelope. You should tell him that in this situation the BEST procedure is to 1.____
   A. make an entry of the sender's name and address in the "missing enclosures" file and forward the letter to its proper destination
   B. return the letter to its sender, attaching a request for the missing enclosure
   C. put the letter aside until a proper investigation may be made concerning the missing enclosure
   D. route the letter to the person for whom it is intended, noting the absence of the enclosure on the letter margin

2. The term "work flow," when used in connection with office management or the activities in an office, GENERALLY means the 2.____
   A. use of charts in the analysis of various office functions
   B. rate of speed at which work flows through a single section of an office
   C. step-by-step physical routing of work through its various procedures
   D. number of individual work units which can be produced by the average employee

3. Physical conditions can have a definite effect on the efficiency and morale of an office. Which of the following statements about physical conditions in an office is CORRECT? 3.____
   A. Hard, non-porous surfaces reflect more noise than linoleum on the top of a desk.
   B. Painting in tints of bright yellow is more appropriate for sunny, well-lit offices than for dark, poorly-lit offices.
   C. Plate glass is better than linoleum for the top of a desk.
   D. The central typing room needs less light than a conference room does.

4. In a certain filing system, documents are consecutively numbered as they are filed, a register is maintained of such consecutively numbered documents, and a record is kept of the number of each document removed from the files and its destination. This system will NOT help in 4.____
   A. finding the present whereabouts of a particular document
   B. proving the accuracy of the data recorded on a certain document
   C. indicating whether observed existing documents were ever filed
   D. locating a desired document without knowing what its contents are

5. In deciding the kind and number of records an agency should keep, the administrative staff must recognize that records are of value in office management PRIMARILY as 5.____

A. informational bases for agency activities
B. data for evaluating the effectiveness of the agency
C. raw material on which statistical analyses are to be based
D. evidence that the agency is carrying out its duties and responsibilities

6. Complaints are often made by the public about the city government's procedures. Although in most cases such procedures cannot be changed since various laws and regulations require them, it may still be possible to reduce the number of complaints. Which one of the following actions by personnel dealing with applicants for city services is LEAST likely to reduce complaints concerning city procedures? 6.____

A. Treating all citizens alike and explaining to them that no exceptions to required procedures can be made
B. Explaining briefly to the citizen why he should comply with regulations
C. Being careful to avoid mistakes which may make additional interviews or correspondence necessary
D. Keeping the citizen informed of the progress of his correspondence when immediate disposition cannot be made

7. In answering a complaint made by a member of the public that a certain essential procedure required by your agency is difficult to follow, it would be BEST for you to stress MOST 7.____

A. that a change in the rules may be considered if enough complaints are received
B. why the operation of a large agency sometimes proves a hardship in individual cases
C. the necessity for the procedure
D. the origin of the procedure

8. When talking to a citizen, it is BEST for an employee of government to 8.____

A. use ordinary conversational phrases and a natural manner
B. try to copy the pronunciation and level of education shown by the citizen
C. try to speak in a very cultured manner and tone
D. use technical terms to show his familiarity with his own work

9. Employees who service the public should maintain an attitude which is both sympathetic and objective.
An UNSYMPATHETIC and SUBJECTIVE attitude would be shown by a public employee who 9.____

A. says "no" with a smile when a citizen's request must be denied
B. listens attentively to a long complaint from a citizen about the government's "red tape"
C. responds with sarcasm when a citizen asks a question which has an obvious answer
D. suggests a definite solution to a citizen's problems

10. You are a supervisor in a city agency and are holding your first interview with a new employee.
In this interview, you should strive MAINLY to 10.____

A. show the new employee that you are an efficient and objective supervisor, with a completely impersonal attitude toward your subordinates
B. complete the entire orientation process including the giving of detailed job-duty instructions
C. make it clear to the employee that all your decisions are based on your many years of experience
D. lay the groundwork for a good employee-supervisor relationship by gaining the new employee's confidence

11. A senior clerk or senior typist may be required to help train a newly-appointed clerk. Which of the following is LEAST important for a newly-appointed clerk to know in order to perform his work efficiently? 11.____

A. Acceptable ways of answering and recording telephone calls
B. The number of files in the storage files unit
C. The filing methods used by his unit
D. Proper techniques for handling visitors

12. In your agency, you have the responsibility of processing clients who have appointments with agency representatives. On a particularly busy day, a client comes to your desk and insists that she must see the person handling her case although she has no appointment.
Under the circumstances, your FIRST action should be to 12.____

A. show her the full appointment schedule
B. give her an appointment for another day
C. ask her to explain the urgency
D. tell her to return later in the day

13. Which of the following practices is BEST for a supervisor to use when assigning work to his staff? 13.____

A. Give workers with seniority the most difficult jobs
B. Assign all unimportant work to the slower workers
C. Permit each employee to pick the job he prefers
D. Make assignments based on the workers' abilities

14. In which of the following instances is a supervisor MOST justified in giving commands to people under his supervision? When 14.____

A. they delay in following instructions which have been given to them clearly
B. they become relaxed and slow about work, and he wants to speed up their production
C. he must direct them in an emergency situation
D. he is instructing them on jobs that are unfamiliar to them

15. Which of the following supervisory actions or attitudes is MOST likely to result in getting subordinates to try to do as much work as possible for a supervisor? He 15.____

A. shows that his most important interest is in schedules and production goals
B. consistently pressures his staff to get the work out
C. never fails to let them know he is in charge
D. considers their abilities and needs while requiring that production goals be met

16. Assume that a senior clerk has been explaining certain regulations to a new clerk under his supervision. 16.____
The MOST efficient way for the senior clerk to make sure that the clerk has understood the explanation is to

A. give him written materials on the regulations
B. ask him if he has any further questions about the regulations
C. ask him specific questions based on what has just been explained to him
D. watch the way he handles a situation involving these regulations

17. One of your unit clerks has been assigned to work for a Mr. Jones in another office for several days. At the end of the first day, Mr. Jones, saying the clerk was not satisfactory, asks that she not be assigned to him again. This clerk is one of your most dependable workers, and no previous complaints about her work have come to you from any other outside assignments. 17.____
To get to the root of this situation, your FIRST action should be to

A. ask Mr. Jones to explain in what way her work was unsatisfactory
B. ask the clerk what she did that Mr. Jones considered unsatisfactory
C. check with supervisors for whom she previously worked to see if your own rating of her is in error
D. tell Mr. Jones to pick the clerk he would prefer to have work for him the next time

18. A senior typist, still on probation, is instructed to type, as quickly as possible, one section of a draft of a long, complex report. Her part must be typed and readable before another part of the report can be written. Asked when she can have the report ready, she gives her supervisor an estimate of a day longer than she knows it will actually take. She then finishes the job a day sooner than the date given her supervisor. 18.____
The judgment shown by a senior typist in giving an overestimate of time in a situation like this is, in general,

A. *good,* because it prevents the supervisor from thinking she works slowly
B. *good,* because it keeps unrealistic supervisors from expecting too much
C. *bad,* because she should have used the time left to further check and proofread her work
D. *bad,* because schedules and plans for other parts of the project may have been based on her false estimate

19. Suppose a new clerk, still on probation, is placed under your supervision and refuses to do a job you ask him to do. 19.____
What is the FIRST thing you should do?

A. Explain that you are the supervisor, and he must follow your instructions.
B. Tell him he may be suspended if he refuses.
C. Ask someone else to do the job, and rate him accordingly.
D. Ask for his reason for objecting to the request.

20. As a supervisor of a small group of people, you have blamed worker A for something that you later find out was really done by worker B. 20.____
The BEST thing for you to do now would be to

   A. say nothing to worker A, but criticize worker B for his mistake while worker A is near so that A will realize that you know who made the mistake
   B. speak to each worker separately, apologize to worker A for your mistake, and discuss worker B's mistake with him
   C. bring both workers together, apologize to worker A for your mistake, and discuss worker B's mistake with him
   D. say nothing new but be careful about mixing up worker A with worker B in the future

21. You have just learned one of your staff is grumbling that she thinks you are not pleased with her work. As far as you are concerned, this is not true at all. In fact, you have paid no particular attention to this worker lately because you have been very busy. You have just finished preparing an important report and "breaking in" a new clerk. 21.____
Under the circumstances, the BEST thing to do is

   A. ignore her; after all, it is just a figment of her imagination
   B. discuss the matter with her now to try to find out and eliminate the cause of this problem
   C. tell her not to worry about it; you have not had time to think about her work
   D. make a note to meet with her at a later date in order to straighten out the situation

22. A most important job of a supervisor is to positively motivate employees to increase their work production. Which of the following LEAST indicates that a group of workers has been positively motivated? 22.____

   A. Their work output becomes constant and stable.
   B. Their cooperation at work becomes greater.
   C. They begin to show pride in the product of their work.
   D. They show increased interest in their work.

23. Which of the following traits would be LEAST important in considering a person for a merit increase? 23.____

   A. Punctuality
   B. Using initiative successfully
   C. High rate of production
   D. Resourcefulness

24. Of the following, the action LEAST likely to gain a supervisor the cooperation of his staff is for him to 24.____

   A. give each person consideration as an individual
   B. be as objective as possible when evaluating work performance
   C. rotate the least popular assignments
   D. expect subordinates to be equally competent

25. It has been said that, for the supervisor, nothing can beat the "face-to-face" communication of talking to one subordinate at a time. 25.____
This method is, however, LEAST appropriate to use when the

A. supervisor is explaining a change in general office procedure
B. subject is of personal importance
C. supervisor is conducting a yearly performance evaluation of all employees
D. supervisor must talk to some of his employees concerning their poor attendance and punctuality

---

KEY (CORRECT ANSWERS)

1.	D	11.	B
2.	C	12.	C
3.	A	13.	D
4.	B	14.	C
5.	A	15.	D
6.	A	16.	C
7.	C	17.	A
8.	A	18.	D
9.	C	19.	D
10.	D	20.	B

21.	B
22.	A
23.	A
24.	D
25.	A

TEST 3

DIRECTIONS: Each question or incomplete statement is followed by several suggested answers or completions. Select the one that BEST answers the question or completes the statement. *PRINT THE LETTER OF THE CORRECT ANSWER IN THE SPACE AT THE RIGHT.*

1. While you are on the telephone answering a question about your agency, a visitor comes to your desk and starts to ask you a question. There is no emergency or urgency in either situation, that of the phone call or that of answering the visitor's question. In this case, you should 1.____

   A. continue to answer the person on the telephone until you are finished and then tell the visitor you are sorry to have kept him waiting
   B. excuse yourself to the person on the telephone and tell the visitor that you will be with him as soon as you have finished on the phone
   C. explain to the person on the telephone that you have a visitor and must shorten the conversation
   D. continue to answer the person on the phone while looking up occasionally at the visitor to let him know that you know he is waiting

2. While speaking on the telephone to someone who called, you are disconnected. The FIRST thing you should do is 2.____

   A. hang up, but try to keep your line free to receive the call back
   B. immediately get the dial tone and continually dial the person who called you until you reach him
   C. signal the switchboard operator and ask her to re-establish the connection
   D. dial "O" for Operator and explain that you were disconnected

3. The type of speech used by an office worker in telephone conversation greatly affects the communication. Of the following, the BEST way to express your ideas when telephoning is with a vocabulary that consists MAINLY of 3.____

   A. formal, intellectual sounding words
   B. often used colloquial words
   C. technical, emphatic words
   D. simple, descriptive words

4. Suppose a clerk under your supervision has taken a personal phone call and is at the same time needed to answer a question regarding an assignment being handled by another member of your office. He appears confused as to what he should do. How should you instruct him later as to how to handle a similar situation? You should tell him to 4.____

   A. tell the caller to hold on while he answers the question
   B. tell the caller to call back a little later
   C. return the call during an assigned break
   D. finish the conversation quickly and answer the question

5. You are asked to place a telephone call by your supervisor. When you place the call, you receive what appears to be a wrong number. Of the following, you should FIRST 5.____

   A. check the number with your supervisor to see if the number he gave you is correct
   B. ask the person on the other end what his number is and who he is
   C. check with the person on the other end to see if the number you dialed is the number you received
   D. apologize to the person on the other end for disturbing him and hang up

6. When you select someone to serve as supervisor of your unit during your absence on vacation and at other times, it would generally be BEST to choose the employee who is 6.____

   A. able to move the work along smoothly, without friction
   B. on staff longest
   C. liked best by the rest of the staff
   D. able to perform the work of each employee to be supervised

7. Successful supervision of handicapped persons employed in a department depends MOST on providing them with a work place and work climate 7.____

   A. which is safe and accident-free
   B. that requires close and direct supervision by others
   C. that requires the performance of routine, repetitive tasks under a minimum of pressure
   D. where they will be accepted by the other employees

8. Studies have indicated that when employees feel that their work is aimless and unchallenging, the allocation or payment of more money for this type of work is likely to 8.____

   A. contribute little to increased production
   B. bring more status to this work
   C. increase employees' feelings of security
   D. give employees greater motivation

9. An employee's performance has fallen below established minimum standards of quantity and quality. The threat of monetary or other disciplinary action as a device for improving this employee's performance would probably be acceptable and MOST effective 9.____

   A. only if applied as soon as the performance fell below standard
   B. only after more constructive techniques have failed
   C. at any time provided the employee understands that the punishment will be carried out
   D. at no time

10. A supervisor must, on short notice, ask his staff to work overtime. Of the following, a technique that is MOST likely to win their willing cooperation would be to 10.____

   A. explain that occasional overtime is part of the job requirement
   B. explain that they will be doing him a personal favor which he will appreciate very much

C. explain why the overtime is necessary
D. promise them that they can take the extra time off in the near future

11. On checking a completed work assignment of an employee, the supervisor finds that the work was not done correctly because the employee had not understood his instructions. Of the following, the BEST way to prevent repetition of this situation next time is for the supervisor to 11.____

A. ask the employee whether he fully understood the instructions and tell him to ask questions in the future whenever anything is unclear
B. ask the employee to repeat the instructions given and test his understanding with several key questions
C. give the instructions a second time, emphasizing the more complicated aspects of the job
D. give work instructions in writing

12. If, as a supervisor, you find yourself pressured for time to handle all of your job responsibilities, the one of the following tasks which it would be MOST appropriate for you to delegate to a subordinate is 12.____

A. attending a staff conference of unit supervisors to discuss the implementation of a new departmental policy
B. making staff work assignments
C. interviewing a new employee
D. checking work of certain employees for accuracy

13. Suppose you are unavoidably late for work one morning. When you arrive at 10 o'clock, you find there are several matters demanding your attention.
Which one of the following matters should you handle LAST? 13.____

A. A visitor who had a 9:30 appointment with you has been waiting to see you since 9 o'clock.
B. An employee on an assignment which should have been completed that morning is absent, and the work will have to be reassigned.
C. Several letters which you dictated at the end of the previous day have been typed and are on your desk for signature and mailing.
D. Your superior called asking you to get certain information for him when you come in and to call him back.

14. Suppose that you have assigned a typist to type a report containing considerable statistical and tabular material and have given her specific instructions as to how this material is to be laid out on each page. When she returns the completed report, you find that it was not prepared according to your instructions, but you may possibly be able to use it the way it was typed. When you question her, she states that she thought her layout was better but you were unavailable for consultation when she began the work.
Of the following, the BEST action for you to take is to 14.____

A. criticize her for not doing the work according to your instructions
B. have her retype the report
C. praise her for her work but tell her she should have waited until she could consult you
D. praise her for using initiative

15. Of the following, the MOST effective way for a supervisor to correct poor work habits of an employee which result in low and poor quality output is to give the employee 15._____

A. additional training
B. less demanding assignments until his work improves
C. continuous supervision
D. more severe criticism

16. Of the following, the BEST way for a supervisor to teach an employee how to do a new and somewhat complicated job is to 16._____

A. assign him to observe another employee who is already skilled in this work and instruct him to consult this employee if he has any questions
B. explain to him how to do it, then demonstrate how it is done, then observe and correct the employee as he does it, then follow up
C. give him a written, detailed, step-by-step explanation of how to do the job and instruct him to ask questions if anything is unclear when he does the work
D. teach him the easiest part of the job first, then the other parts one at a time, in order of their difficulty, as the employee masters the easier parts

17. After an employee has completed telling his supervisor about a grievance against a co-worker, the supervisor tells the employee that he will take action to remove the cause of the grievance. 17._____
The action of the supervisor was

A. *good,* because ill feeling between subordinates interferes with proper performance
B. *poor,* because the supervisor should give both employees time to "cool off"
C. *good,* because grievances that appear petty to the supervisor are important to subordinates
D. *poor,* because the supervisor should tell the employee that he will investigate the matter before he comes to any conclusion

18. During work on an important project, one employee in a secretarial pool turns in several pages of typed copy, one page of which contains several errors. 18._____
Of these four comments which her supervisor might possibly make, which one would be MOST constructive?

A. "You did such a poor job on this; I will have to have it done over."
B. "You will have to do better,more consistently than this,if you want to be in charge of a secretarial pool yourself someday."
C. "How come you made so many mistakes here? Your other pages were all right."
D. "If my boss saw this, he would be very displeased with you."

19. A supervisor has general supervision over a large, complex project with many employees. The work is subdivided among small units of employees, each with a senior clerk or senior stenographer in charge. At a staff meeting, after all work assignments have been made, the supervisor tells all the employees that they are to take orders only from their immediate supervisor and instructs them to let him know if anyone else tries to give them orders. 19._____
This instruction by the supervising clerk is

A. *good,* because it may prevent the issuance of orders by unauthorized persons, which would interfere with the accomplishment of the assignment
B. *poor,* because employees should be instructed to take up such problems with their immediate supervisor
C. *good,* because orders issued by immediate supervisors would be precise and directly related to the tasks of the assignments while those issued by others would not be
D. *poor,* because it places upon all employees a responsibility which should not normally be theirs

20. A supervisor who is to direct a team of senior clerks and clerks in a complex project, calls them together beforehand to inform them of the tasks each employee will perform on this job. 20.____
Of the following, the CHIEF value of this action by the supervisor is that each member of this team will be able to

A. work independently in the absence of the supervisor
B. understand what he will do and how this will fit into the total picture
C. share in the process of decision-making as an equal participant
D. judge how well the plans for this assignment have been made

21. A supervisor who has both younger and older employees under his supervision may sometimes find that employee absenteeism seriously interferes with accomplishment of goals. 21.____
Studies of such employee absenteeism have shown that the absences of employees

A. under 35 years of age are usually unexpected and the absences of employees over 45 years of age are usually unnecessary
B. of all age groups show the same characteristics as to length of absence
C. under 35 years of age are for frequent, short periods while the absences of employees over 45 years of age are less frequent but of longer duration
D. under 35 years of age are for periods of long duration and the absences of employees over 45 years of age are for periods of short duration

22. Suppose you have a long-standing procedure for getting a certain job done by your subordinates that is apparently a good one. Changes in some steps of the procedure are made from time to time to handle special problems that come up. 22.____
For you to review this procedure periodically is desirable MAINLY because

A. the system is working well
B. checking routines periodically is a supervisor's chief responsibility
C. subordinates may be confused as to how the procedure operates as a result of the changes made
D. it is necessary to determine whether the procedure has become outdated or is in need of improvement

23. Suppose that a stranger enters the office you are in charge of and asks for the address and telephone number of one of your employees. 23.____
Of the following, it would be BEST for you to

A. find out why he needs the information and release it if his reason is a good one
B. explain that you are not permitted to release such information to unauthorized persons

C. give him the information but tell him it must be kept confidential
D. ask him to leave the office immediately

24. A member of the public approaches an employee who is at work at his desk. The employee cannot interrupt his work in order to take care of this person. Of the following, the BEST and MOST courteous way of handling this situation is for the employee to 24.____

A. avoid looking up from his work until he is finished with what he is doing
B. tell this person that he will not be able to take care of him for quite a while
C. refer the individual to another employee who can take care of him right away
D. chat with the individual while he continues with his work

25. You answer a phone call from a citizen who urgently needs certain information you do not have, but you think you know who may have it. He is angry because he has already been switched to two different offices. Of the following, it would be BEST for you to 25.____

A. give him the phone number of the person you think may have the information he wants, but explain you are not sure
B. tell him you regret you cannot help him because you are not sure who can give him the information
C. advise him that the best way he can be sure of getting the information he wants is to write a letter to the agency
D. get the phone number where he can be reached and tell him you will try to get the information he wants and will call him back later

---

KEY (CORRECT ANSWERS)

1. B
2. A
3. D
4. C
5. C
6. A
7. D
8. A
9. B
10. C
11. B
12. D
13. C
14. A
15. A
16. B
17. D
18. C
19. B
20. B
21. C
22. D
23. B
24. C
25. D

EXAMINATION SECTION

TEST 1

DIRECTIONS: Each question or incomplete statement is followed by several suggested answers or completions. Select the one that BEST answers the question or completes the statement. *PRINT THE LETTER OF THE CORRECT ANSWER IN THE SPACE AT THE RIGHT.*

1. From time to time, your subordinates are assigned to other units to do reception work and other duties. You receive a note from Mr. Jones, the head of one of these other units, stating that the work of Miss Smith, one of your subordinates, was unsatisfactory when she worked for him, and asking you not to assign her to him again. Although Miss Smith has worked in your unit for a long time, this is the first time that anyone has complained about her work. 1.____
The one of the following actions that you should take FIRST in this situation is to ask
   A. the heads of the other units for whom Miss Smith has worked whether or not her work has been satisfactory
   B. Mr. Jones in what way Miss Smith's work has been unsatisfactory
   C. Miss Smith to explain in what way her work for Mr. Jones was unsatisfactory
   D. Mr. Jones which of your subordinates he would prefer to have assigned to him

2. Suppose that you are the supervisor of a small unit in a city agency. You have given one of your subordinates, Mr. Smith, an assignment which must be completed by the end of the day. Because he is unfamiliar with the assignment, Mr. Smith will be unable to complete it on time. Your other subordinates are too busy to help Mr. Smith, but you have the time to help him complete the assignment. 2.____
For you to help Mr. Smith complete the assignment would be
   A. *desirable*; because a supervisor is expected to be familiar with his subordinates' work
   B. *undesirable*; because Mr. Smith will come to depend on you to help him do his work
   C. *desirable*; because Mr. Smith is likely to appreciate your help and give you his cooperation when you need it
   D. *undesirable*; because a supervisor should not perform the same type of work as his subordinates do

3. For a supervisor to listen to the personal problems which his subordinates bring to him is GENERALLY 3.____
   A. *desirable*; it is likely that the supervisor has broader experience in solving personal problems than do his subordinates
   B. *undesirable*; the supervisor may be unable to solve such problems

C. *desirable*; the supervisor can better understand his subordinates' behavior on the job
D. *undesirable*; permitting a subordinate to talk about his personal problems may only make them seem worse

4. A generally accepted concept of management is that the authority given to a person should be commensurate with his 4.____
A. responsibility
B. ability
C. seniority
D. dependability

5. It has been said that the best supervisor is the one who gives the fewest orders. The one of the following supervisor practices that would be MOT likely to increase the number of orders that a supervisor must give to get out the work is to 5.____
A. set general goals for his subordinates and give them the authority for reaching the goals
B. train subordinates to make decisions for themselves
C. establish routines for his subordinates' jobs
D. introduce frequent changes in the work methods his subordinates are using

6. The one of the following supervisory practices that would be MOST likely to give subordinates a feeling of satisfaction in their work is to 6.____
A. establish work goals that take a long time to achieve
B. show the subordinates how their work goals are related to the goals of the agency
C. set work goals higher than the subordinates can achieve
D. refrain from telling the subordinates that they are failing to meet their work goals

7. You are about to design a system for measuring the quantity of work produced by your subordinates. 7.____
The one of the following which is the FIRST step that you should take in designing this system is to
A. establish the units of work measurement to be used in the system
B. determine the actual advantages and disadvantages of the system
C. determine the abilities of each of your subordinates
D. ascertain the types of work done in the unit

8. One of your subordinates tells you that he is dissatisfied with his work assignment and that he wishes to discuss the matter with you. The employee is obviously very angry and upset. 8.____
Of the following, the course of action that you should take FIRST in this situation is to
A. postpone discussion of the employee's complaint, explaining to him that the matter can be settled more satisfactorily if it is discussed calmly
B. have the employee describe his complaint, correcting him whenever he makes what seems to be an erroneous charge against you

C. permit the employee to present his complaint in full, withholding your comments until he has finished describing his complaint
D. promise the employee that you will review all the work assignments in the unit to determine whether or not any changes should be made

9. Assume that you are the supervisor of a unit in a city agency. One of your subordinates has violated an important rule of the agency. For such a violation, you are required to impose discipline in the form of a reprimand given in private. 9.____
Of the following, the MOST important reason for disciplining the employee for violating the rule is to
A. obtain his compliance with the rule
B. punish him for his action in an impartial manner
C. establish your authority to administer discipline
D. impress upon all the employees in the unit the need for observing the rule

10. You are the newly appointed supervisor of a small unit in a city agency. One of your subordinates, Mr. Smith, a competent employee, has resented your appointment as his supervisor and has not been as cooperative toward you as you have wanted him to be. One day, Mr. Smith fails to observe an important rule of the agency. You are required to reprimand any employee who fails to observe the rule. 10.____
The one of the following courses of action you should take in this situation is to
A. attempt to overcome Mr. Smith's resentment by explaining to him that although you should reprimand him, you will not do so
B. reprimand Mr. Smith after pointing out to him that he failed to observe the rule
C. tell Mr. Smith that if he becomes more cooperative, you will overlook his failure to observe the rule
D. tell Mr. Smith that although you did not originate the rule, nevertheless you are required to reprimand him

11. Suppose that a clerk who has injured himself on the job because of his carelessness informs his supervisor of the accident. The supervisor has been newly appointed to his job and is anxious to keep accidents at a minimum. The action taken by the supervisor is to criticize the subordinate for his carelessness and to tell him that he is holding him responsible for the accident. 11.____
Of the following, it would be MOST reasonable to conclude that, as a result of the supervisor's action, his subordinates may
A. tend to withhold information from him about future accidents
B. be critical of him, in turn, if he himself is injured on the job
C. expect him to supervise them more closely in the future
D. attempt to correct hazardous job conditions without his knowledge

12. The one of the following which is GENERALLY the basic reason for using standard procedures in an agency is to 12.____
A. provide sequences of steps for handling recurring activities
B. facilitate periodic review of standard practices

C. train new employees in the agency's policies and objectives
D. serve as a basis for formulating agency policies

13. Assume that the operations of a certain unit in an agency enable the supervisor to allow each of his subordinates wide discretion in selecting the kind and amount of work he chooses to do. However, in evaluating the work of his subordinates, the supervisor places more emphasis on some area of work than on others. Factors such as number of applications processed and number of letters written are given great weight in evaluation, while factors such as number of papers filed and number of forms checked are given little weight. Hence, a subordinate who processes a large number of applications would receive a high evaluation even if he checked very few forms. 13.____
The supervisor's method of evaluation would MOST likely result in a(n)
A. increase in the amount of time spent on processing each application
B. backlog of papers waiting to be filed
C. improvement in the quality of letters written
D. decline in output in all areas of work

14. Some management authorities propose that work assignments be made by assigning a varied set of tasks to a group of employees and then allowing the group to decide for itself how to organize the work to be done. This method of assigning work is called *job enlargement*. 14.____
The one of the following which is considered to be the CHIEF advantage of job enlargement is that it
A. encourages employees to specialize in the work they are assigned to do
B. reduces the amount of control that employees have over their work
C. increases the employees' job satisfaction
D. reduces the number of skills that each employee is required to learn

15. In conducting a meeting to pass along information to his subordinates, a supervisor may talk to his subordinates without giving them the opportunity to interrupt him. This method is called one-way communication. On the other hand, the supervisor may talk to his subordinates and give them the opportunity to ask questions or make comments while he is speaking. This method is called two-way communication. 15.____
It would be MORE desirable for the supervisor to use two-way communication rather than one-way communication at a meeting when his primary purpose is to
A. avoid, during the meeting, open criticism of any mistakes he may make
B. conduct the meeting in an orderly fashion
C. pass along information quickly
D. transmit information which must be clearly understood

16. Assume that you are the leader of a training conference on supervisory techniques and problems. One of the participants in the conference proposes what you consider to be an unsatisfactory technique for handling the problem under discussion. 16.____

The one of the following courses of action which you should take in this situation is to

A. explain to the participants why the proposed technique is unsatisfactory
B. stimulate the other participants to discuss the appropriateness of the proposed technique
C. proceed immediately to another problem without discussing the proposed technique
D. end further discussion of the problem but explain to the participant in private, after the conference is over, why he proposed technique is unsatisfactory

17. In measuring the work of his subordinates, the supervisor of a unit performing routine filing began by observing his subordinates at work. If a subordinate seemed to be busy, then the supervisor concluded that the subordinate was producing a great deal of work. On the other hand, the supervisor concluded that a subordinate was not producing much work if he did not seem to be busy. The supervisor's work measurement method was faulted CHIEFLY because 17.____

A. it did not use a standard against which a subordinate's work could be measured
B. the type of work performed by his subordinates did not lend itself to accurate measurement
C. his subordinates may not have worked at their normal rates if they were aware that their work was being observed
D. the supervisor may not have observed a subordinate's work for a long enough period of time

18. Assume that a system of statistical reports designed to provide information about employee work performance is put into effect in a unit of a city agency. There is some evidence that the employees of this unit are working below their capacities. The information obtained from the system is to be used by management to improve employee work and performance and to evaluate such performance. The employees whose work is to be recorded by the reports resent them. Nevertheless, the employees' work performance improves substantially after the reporting system is put into effect, and before management has put the information to use.
The one of the following which is the MOST accurate conclusion to be drawn from this situation is that 18.____

A. a statistical reporting system may fail to provide the information it is designed to provide
B. low employee morale may have been the cause of the employees' former level of work performance
C. a statistical reporting system designed only to provide information about problems may also help to solve the problems
D. willing employee cooperation is essential to the success of a system of statistical reports

19. In setting the work standard for a certain task, a unit supervisor took the total output of all the employees in the unit and divided it by the number of employees. He thus established the average output as the work standard for the task. 19.____
The method that the supervisor used to establish the work standard is GENERALLY considered to be
A. *proper,* since the method takes into account the output of the outstanding, as well as of the less productive, employees
B. *improper*, since the average output may not be what could reasonably be expected of a competent, satisfactory employee
C. *proper*, since the standard is based on the actual output of the employees who are to be evaluated
D. *improper*, since all the employees in the unit may be successful in meeting the work standard

20. There are disadvantages as well as advantages in using statistical controls to measure specific aspects of subordinates' jobs. 20.____
The one of the following which can LEAST be considered to be an advantage of statistical controls to a supervisor is that such controls may
A. reduce the need for close, detailed supervision
B. give the supervisor information that he needs for making decisions
C. stimulate subordinates whose work is measured by statistical controls to improve their performance
D. encourage subordinates to emphasize aspects being measured rather than their jobs as a whole

21. Mr. Stone, who has been recently placed in charge of a clerical unit staffed with ten employees, plans to institute several radical changes in the procedures of his unit. 21.____
Of the following actions he may take before adopting any of the revisions, the MOST desirable one is for Mr. Stone to
A. distribute to each staff member a memorandum describing the revised procedures and requesting the staff's cooperation in giving the revised procedures a fair trial
B. issue to each staff member a memorandum describing the proposed changes and inviting him to submit his written criticism of these proposed changes
C. issue to each staff member a memorandum describing the proposed changes and notifying him of the time and date of a staff conference to be held on the merits
D. of the proposed changes discuss the proposed changes with each staff member independently and obtain his opinion of the proposed changes

22. An assignment completed by Frank King is returned to him by his unit supervisor for certain changes. Frank King objects to making these changes. 22.____
Of the following, the MOST appropriate action for the unit supervisor to take FIRST is to
A. permit Frank King to present his arguments against making these changes

B. inform Frank King that he is free to take the matter up with a higher authority
C. reprimand Frank King for objecting and assign another employee to make these changes
D. state briefly that his decision is final and indicate by his manner that further discussion would be useless

23. Of the following, it is LEAST essential for a supervisor, in assigning work to a subordinate, to issue written instructions when the 23.____
A. supervisor will be on hand to check the work
B. instructions are to be passed on to other employees
C. assignment involves many details
D. subordinate is to be held strictly accountable for the work performed

24. Assume that you have been placed in charge of a unit where the quality of the work performed is poor. You plan to discuss the matter of improving the quality of the wok at a staff meeting of the unit. 24.____
Of the following courses of action which you might take at this meeting, the BEST one is to
A. describe a few cases of exceptionally poor work performance; then have the employees performing this work explain why their work was done poorly
B. inform the staff that you will be criticized by your own superior if the quality of the unit's work does not improve; then discuss, in general terms, the problem of improving the quality of the work
C. discuss the problem of improving the quality of the unit's work; then call upon each employee by name for his suggestions for improving the work he performs
D. present the problem to the staff; then indicate and discuss specific methods for improving the quality of the work

25. Suppose that certain office responsibilities require you to be frequently absent from the unit you supervise. You have, therefore, decided to designate one of your staff members to act as unit head in your absence. 25.____
Of the following factors, the one which is MOST important in selecting the employee best fitted for this assignment is his
A. manner and personal appearance
B. estimated ability to perform work of a supervisory nature
C. ability to perform his present duties
D. relative seniority in the service

KEY (CORRECT ANSWERS)

1.	B	11.	A
2.	C	12.	A
3.	C	13.	B
4.	A	14.	C
5.	D	15.	D
6.	B	16.	B
7.	D	17.	A
8.	C	18.	C
9.	A	19.	B
10.	B	20.	D

21.	C
22.	A
23.	A
24.	D
25.	B

TEST 2

DIRECTIONS: Each question or incomplete statement is followed by several suggested answers or completions. Select the one that BEST answers the question or completes the statement. *PRINT THE LETTER OF THE CORRECT ANSWER IN THE SPACE AT THE RIGHT.*

1. Assume that your supervisor has placed you in complete charge of an important project and that several clerks have been assigned to assist you. You have been given authority to establish any new procedures or revise existing procedures in order to complete the project as soon as possible. Just before you begin work on the project, one of the clerks suggests a change in the procedure which you realize at once would result in completion of the project in about half the time you expected to spend on it. 1.____
Of the following, the MOST effective course of action for you to take is to
   A. adopt the suggestion immediately to expedite the completion of the project
   B. discuss the suggestion with your superior to obtain his consent to the change
   C. point out to the clerk that an adequate procedure has already been established, but that his suggestion may be used in future projects of this type
   D. encourage the other clerks to make further suggestions

2. A supervisor of a unit may safely delegate certain of his functions to his subordinates. 2.____
Of the following, the function which can MOST safely be delegated is the
   A. settlement of employee grievances
   B. planning and scheduling of the production of the unit
   C. improvement of production methods of the unit
   D. maintenance of records of the work output of the unit

3. Some organizations now question the effectiveness of extreme job specialization. It is felt that in some instances it may be more advantageous to enlarge the scope of individual jobs, thus providing the employee with a greater variety of tasks. 3.____
Of the following, the one which is LEAST likely to be a result of enlarging the scope of jobs is a(n)
   A. increase in the employee's job responsibilities
   B. decrease in the number of job titles in the organization
   C. increase in the number of tasks performed by an employee
   D. decrease in employee flexibility

4. A manual that is essentially designed to present detailed procedures and policies is not necessarily a good training medium, nor is a manual designed for high-level administrators likely to be satisfactory for use at lower levels. 4.____
The MOST valid implication of this quotation is that
   A. a manual, to be effective, should be flexible enough to apply to any working level in an organization

B. the uses to which a manual will be put and the people who will use it should be carefully determined before it is prepared
C. the more detailed procedures a manual contains, the more effective it will be for the use of administrators
D. the degree of difficulty encountered in the preparation of a manual varies with the purpose for which it is designed and the people for whom it is written

5. In assigning a complicated task to a group of subordinates, Mr. Jones, a unit supervisor, neither indicates the specific steps to be followed in performing the assignment nor designates the subordinate to be responsible for seeing that the task is done on time. 5.____
This supervisor's method of assigning the task is MOST likely to result in
A. the loss of skills previously acquired by his subordinates
B. assumption of authority by the most capable subordinates
C. friction and misunderstanding among subordinates with consequent delays in work
D. greater individual effort and self-reliance on the part of his subordinates

6. Assume that the head of your agency has appointed you to a committee that has been assigned the task of reviewing the clerical procedures used in a large bureau of the agency and of recommending appropriate changes in the procedures where necessary. 6.____
Of the following, the FIRST step that should be taken by the committee in carrying out its assignment is to
A. survey the most efficient procedures used in comparable agencies
B. study the organization of the bureau and the work it is required to do
C. evaluate the possible effects of proposed revisions in the procedures
D. determine the effectiveness of existing procedures

7. A recently developed practice in administration favors reducing the number of levels of authority in an organization, increasing the number of subordinates reporting to a superior, and also increasing the authority delegated to the subordinates. 7.____
This practice would MOST likely result in a(n)
A. increase in the span of control exercised by superiors
B. increase in detailed information that flows to a superior from each subordinate
C. decrease in the responsibility exercised by the subordinates
D. decrease in the number of functions performed by the subordinates

8. As an organization grows larger, the amount of personal contact between the top administrative officials and the rank and file employees diminishes. Consequently, management comes to rely more heavily upon written reports and records for securing information and exercising control. 8.____
The MOST valid implication of this quotation is that, as an organization grows larger,
A. evaluation of the work of rank and file employees becomes more objective because of greater reliance upon written reports and records

B. relations between first-line supervisors and their subordinates grow more impersonal
C. top administrative officials depend upon less direct methods for controlling the work of their subordinates
D. it becomes more difficult for top administrative officials to maintain high morale among rank and file employees

9. A supervisor whose unit has a good production record is usually found to be more occupied with the functions associated with leadership than with the performance of the same functions as his subordinates. 9.____
The MOST valid implication of this quotation is that
A. a supervisor whose unit has a good production record usually is not as competent in performing routine tasks as are his subordinates
B. ability to lead and competence in performing the day-to-day tasks of his subordinates are the requirements of a successful supervisor
C. a supervisor who spends more time on planning and organizing the work of his unit than on performing the routine tasks of his subordinates will find that a his unit's production record will be good
D. a supervisor whose unit has a good production record usually places less emphasis on performing the day-to-day tasks of his subordinates than on planning the work of his unit

10. To delegate work is one of the main functions of the supervisor. In delegating work, the supervisor should remember that even though an assignment is delegated to a subordinate, the supervisor ultimately is responsible for seeing that the work is done. 10.____
The MOST valid implication of this quotation for a supervisor is that he should
A. delegate as few difficult tasks as possible so as to minimize the consequences of inadequate performance by his subordinates
B. delegate to his subordinates those tasks which he considers difficult or time-consuming
C. check the progress of delegated assignments periodically to make certain that the work is being done properly
D. assign work to a subordinate without holding him directly accountable for carrying it out

11. A supervisor should select and develop an understudy to take charge of the unit in the supervisor's absence and to assist the supervisor whenever necessary. 11.____
Of the following, the technique that would be LEAST effective in developing an understudy is for the supervisor to
A. permit him to exercise complete supervision over certain parts of the work
B. assign him to work in which there is little likelihood of his making mistakes, so as to increase his self-confidence
C. accustom him to making reports on the progress of work he is supervising
D. give him responsibility gradually so that he will have time to absorb each new responsibility

12. A procedure manual of an agency is potentially more usable than are files of individual messages or bulletins, but usability and usefulness are not routine by-products of the manual form. 12.____
The MOST valid implication of this is that
   A. the purpose of a manual should not be confined to an explanation of routine procedures
   B. a manual may prove to be unsuitable for some of its anticipated uses
   C. individual messages or bulletins are more likely to be of use than are manuals
   D. a manual suffers from certain limitations that are not found in individual messages or bulletins

13. As the supervisor of a unit in an agency, you have just been instructed to put into effect a new procedure which you know will be disliked by your subordinates. 13.____
Of the following, the MOST important reason for calling a meeting of your staff before putting the new procedure into effect is to
   A. help you to determine which workers will be reluctant to cooperate in carrying out the new procedure
   B. allow you to announce that the new procedure must be put into effect despite any objections which might be raised
   C. enable you to explain that you don't approve of the new procedure and to give the reasons why it must nevertheless be put into effect
   D. permit you to discuss the purpose of the new procedure and to present the reasons for its adoption

14. Assume that you are a training conference leader and that you have just begun a series of conferences on supervisory techniques for new supervisors. Each conference is scheduled to last for three hours. A thorough discussion of all the material planned for the first session, which you had estimated would last until 4 P.M., is completed by 3:30 P.M. 14.____
For you to summarize the points that have been made and close the meeting would be
   A. *advisable*; the participants will lose interest in the conference if it is permitted to continue merely to occupy the remaining time
   B. *inadvisable*; the participants should be asked if there are any other topics that they would like to discuss
   C. *advisable*; the participants in a training conference should not be kept from their regular work for long periods of time
   D. *inadvisable*; material scheduled for discussion at future sessions should be used for the remainder of this session

15. In any agency, the top administrative officials are concerned largely with the work of overall creative planning with respect to the anticipated progress of the agency. The first-line supervisors, on the other hand, are concerned largely with the control of current action for the execution of current jobs. 15.____
On the basis of this quotation, a first-line supervisor would be CHIEFLY responsible for

A. increasing or decreasing the responsibilities of his unit to reflect changes in the policies of the agency
B. modifying the work assignments of his present staff to handle a seasonal variation in the activities of the unit
C. revising the procedure that is used for transmitting instructions from the head of the agency to the unit heads
D. raising and lowering the production goals of his unit as often as necessary to adjust them to the abilities of his subordinates

16. The control of clerical work in an agency appears impossible if the clerical work is regarded merely as a series of duties unrelated to the functions of the agency. However, this control becomes feasible when it is realized that clerical work links and coordinates the functions of the agency. 16.____
On the basis of this quotation, the MOST accurate of the following statements is that the
A. complexity of clerical work may not be fully understood by those assigned to control it
B. clerical work can be readily controlled if it is coordinated by other work of the agency
C. number of clerical tasks may be reduced by regarding coordination as the function of clerical work
D. purposes of clerical work must be understood to make possible its proper control

17. Assume that as supervisor of a unit you are to prepare a vacation schedule for the employees in your unit. 17.____
Of the following, the factor which is LEAST important for you to consider in setting up this schedule is
A. the vacation preferences of each employee in the unit
B. the anticipated workload in the unit during the vacation period
C. how well each employee has performed his work
D. how essential a specific employee's services will be during the vacation period

18. In order to promote efficiency and economy in an agency, it is advisable for the management systematize and standardize procedures and relationships insofar as this can be done; however, excessive routinizing which does not permit individual contributions or achievements should be avoided. 18.____
On the basis of this quotation, it is MOST accurate to state that
A. systematized procedures should be designed mainly to encourage individual achievements
B. standardized procedures should allow for individual accomplishments
C. systematization of procedures may not be possible in organizations which have a large variety of functions
D. individual employees of an organization must fully accept standardized procedures if the procedures are to be effective

19. Trained employees work most efficiently and with a minimum expenditure of time and energy. Suitable equipment and definite, well-developed procedures are effective only when employees know how to use the equipment and procedures. 19.____
This quotation means MOST NEARLY that
   A. employees can be trained most efficiently when suitable equipment and definite procedures are used
   B. training of employees is a costly but worthwhile investment
   C. suitable equipment and definite procedures are of greatest value when employees have been properly traced to use them
   D. the cost of suitable equipment and definite procedures is negligible when the saving in time and energy that they bring is considered

20. Assume that your supervisor has asked you to present to him comprehensive, periodic reports on the progress that your unit is making in meeting its work goals. 20.____
For you to give your superior oral reports rather than written ones is
   A. *desirable*; it will be easier for him to transmit your oral reports to his superiors
   B. *undesirable*; the oral reports will provide no permanent record to which he may refer
   C. *undesirable*; there will be less opportunity for you to discuss the oral reports with him than the written ones
   D. *desirable*; the oral reports will require little time and effort to prepare

21. Assume that an employee under your supervision complains to you that your evaluation of his work is too low. 21.____
The MOST appropriate action for you to take FIRST is to
   A. explain how you arrived at the evaluation of his work
   B. encourage him to improve the quality of his work by pointing out specifically how he can do so
   C. suggest that he appeal to an impartial higher authority if he disagrees with your evaluation
   D. point out to him specific instances in which his work has been unsatisfactory

22. The nature of the experience and education that are made a prerequisite to employment determines in large degree the training job to be done after employment begins. 22.____
On the basis of this quotation, it is MOST accurate to state that
   A. the more comprehensive the experience and education required for employment, the more extensive the training that is usually given after appointment
   B. the training that is given to employees depends upon the experience and education required of them before appointment
   C. employees who possess the experience and education required for employment should need little additional training after appointment
   D. the nature of the work that employees are expected to perform determines the training that they will need

23. Assume that you are preparing a report evaluating the work of a clerk who was transferred to your unit from another unit in the agency about a year ago. 23.____
Of the following, the method that would probably be MOST helpful to you in making this evaluation is to
   A. consult the evaluations this employee received from his former supervisors
   B. observe this employee at his work for a week shortly before you prepare the report
   C. examine the employee's production records and compare them with the standards set for the position
   D. obtain tactfully from his fellow employees their frank opinions of his work

24. Of the following, the CHIEF value of a flow of work chart to the management of an organization is its usefulness in 24.____
   A. locating the causes of delay in carrying out an operation
   B. training new employees in the performance of their duties
   C. determining the effectiveness of the employees in the organization
   D. determining the accuracy of its organization chart

25. Assume that a procedure for handling certain office forms has just been extensively revised. As supervisor of a small unit, you are to instruct your subordinates in the use of the new procedure, which is rather complicated. 25.____
Of the following, it would be LEAST helpful to your subordinates for you to
   A. compare the revised procedure with the one it has replaced
   B. state that you believe the revised procedure to be better than the one it has replaced
   C. tell them that they will probably find it difficult to learn the new procedure
   D. give only a general outline of the revised procedure at first and then follow with more detailed instructions

KEY (CORRECT ANSWERS)

1. A
2. D
3. D
4. B
5. C

6. B
7. A
8. C
9. D
10. C

11. B
12. B
13. D
14. A
15. B

16. B
17. C
18. B
19. C
20. B

21. A
22. B
23. C
24. A
25. C

TEST 3

DIRECTIONS: Each question or incomplete statement is followed by several suggested answers or completions. Select the one that BEST answers the question or completes the statement. *PRINT THE LETTER OF THE CORRECT ANSWER IN THE SPACE AT THE RIGHT.*

1. A methods improvement program might be called a war against habit. The MOST accurate implication of this statement is that 1.____
   A. routine handling of routine office assignments should be discouraged
   B. standardization of office procedures may encourage employees to form inefficient work habits
   C. employees tend to continue the use of existing procedures, even when such procedures are inefficient
   D. procedures should be changed consistently to prevent them from becoming habits

2. An office supervisor may give either a written or an oral order to his subordinates when making an assignment. 2.____
   Of the following, it would be MOST appropriate for a supervisor to issue an order in writing when
   A. a large number of two-page reports must be stapled together before the end of the day
   B. the assignment is to be completed within two hours after it is issued to his subordinates
   C. his subordinates have completed an identical assignment the day before
   D. several entries must be made on a form at varying intervals of time by different clerks

3. A supervisor should always remember that the instruction or training of new employees is most effective if it is given when and where it is needed. 3.____
   On the basis of this quotation, it is MOST appropriate to conclude that
   A. the new employee should be trained to handle any aspect of his work at the time he starts his job
   B. the new employee should be given the training essential to get him started and additional training when he requires it
   C. an employee who has received excessive training will be just as ineffective as one who has received inadequate training
   D. a new employee is trained most effectively by his own supervisor

4. A supervisor may make assignments to his subordinates in the form of a command, a request, or a call for volunteers. 4.____
   It is LEAST desirable for a supervisor to make an assignment in the form of a command when
   A. a serious emergency has risen
   B. an employee objects to carrying out an assignment
   C. the assignment must be completed immediately
   D. the assignment is an unpleasant one

5. For an office supervisor to confer periodically with his subordinates in order to anticipate job problems which are likely to arise is desirable MAINLY because 5.____
   A. there will be fewer problems for which hasty decisions will have to be made
   B. some problems which are anticipated may not arise
   C. his subordinates will learn to refer the problems arising in the unit to him
   D. constant anticipation of future problems tends to raise additional problems

6. As the supervisor of a staff of clerical employees performing various types of work, you are responsible for the accuracy and efficiency with which their work is performed. 6.____
   Of the following actions you may take to insure the accuracy of their work, the MOST practical one is for you to
   A. review each operation completed by a staff member before permitting the employee to proceed to the next operation
   B. keep a record of every error made by an employee and use this record to determine whether a careless employee should be transferred or discharged
   C. assign work in such a way that every operation is performed independently by two employees
   D. determine what errors are likely to occur and set up safeguards to prevent the occurrence of these errors

7. One of your subordinates has violated a staff regulation by failing to inform you that he will be absent on a certain day. 7.____
   Of the following, the MOST appropriate action for you to take FIRST is to
   A. discuss this matter with your immediate superior
   B. find out the reason for his failure to obey this staff regulation
   C. determine what disciplinary action other supervisors have taken in similar cases
   D. take no action if his absence did not interfere with the work of the unit; reprimand him if it did

8. A newly appointed clerk is assigned to a unit of an agency at a time when the supervisor of the unit is very busy and has little time to devote to instructing the new employee in the work he is to perform. 8.____
   Of the following, the MOST appropriate method of training this employee is for the supervisor to
   A. instruct the new employee to observe several experienced clerks at work and question them regarding any aspect of the work he does not understand
   B. delegate the job of training this employee to an employee in the unit who is qualified to instruct him
   C. assign the new employee a simple task and inform him that more complex and varied duties will be given him when the supervisor is less busy
   D. have the employee spend his time reading the agency's annual reports and the laws, rules, and regulations governing its work

9. The channels of communication between the management of a bureau and its employees not only should be kept open and working, but they should also be two-way channels. 9.____
Of the following, the MOST effective method for a supervisor to use to carry out this recommendation is to
   A. arrange periodic staff meetings and individual conferences to discuss problems and procedures with his subordinates
   B. change subordinates' assignments regularly so that they will be able to see how their work is related to the objectives of the bureau
   C. issue regular instructions, both written and oral, which clearly show each subordinate's assignments
   D. encourage his subordinates to discuss personal problems with him

10. Work measurement is an essential control tool to an office supervisor. 10.____
Of the following, the LEAST important reason for using work measurement as a control tool is that work measurement
   A. may indicate training needs of his subordinates
   B. simplifies the procedures used by the supervisor's subordinates in carrying out their assignments
   C. can indicate whether the supervisor is employing more subordinates than he really needs
   D. is a basis for determining which of the supervisor's subordinates are his most efficient

11. Internal management reporting in agencies is becoming more statistical in nature. Statistics have thus become a major tool in management supervision in agencies. 11.____
Before deciding to adopt statistical reporting as a management tool, the management of an agency should FIRST determine whether the
   A. employees of the agency understand the need for, and the use of, statistics in reporting
   B. supervisory staff in the agency is capable of putting reports into statistical form
   C. major activities of the agency can be reported statistically
   D. present achievements of the agency can be compared statistically with those of previous years

12. When assigning work, which of the following criteria would be BEST for a supervisor to use? 12.____
   A. Allow each employee to select the tasks he or she does best
   B. Assign all unimportant work to the slower employees
   C. Assign the more tiring tasks to the newer employees
   D. Assign tasks based on the abilities of employees

13. You have been supervising ten people for sixteen months. During that time, your employees have never reported any problems to you. 13.____
It is LIKELY that
   A. you are doing such a good job there is no room for improvement

B. since your staff is small, the chances of problems arising are smaller than in a larger unit
C. for some reason your staff is reluctant to discuss problems with you
D. your employees are very competent and are handling all of the problems well by themselves

14. Your supervisor informs you that three of your fifteen employees have complained to her about your inconsistent methods of supervision. 14.____
You should
A. offer to attend a supervisory training program
B. first ask her if it is proper for her to allow these employees to go over your head
C. ask her what specific acts have been considered inconsistent
D. explain that you have purposely been inconsistent because of the needs of these three employees

15. On short notice, a supervisor must ask her staff to work overtime. 15.____
Of the following, it would be BEST to
A. explain they would be doing her a personal favor which she would appreciate a great deal
B. explain why it is necessary
C. reassure them that they can take the time off in the near future
D. remind them that working overtime occasionally is part of the job requirement

16. One of your employees has begun reporting to work late on the average of twice a week. 16.____
You should
A. send a memo to everyone in your unit, stressing that lateness cannot be tolerated
B. privately discuss the matter with the employee to determine if there are any unusual circumstances causing the behavior
C. bring the issue up at the next staff meeting, without singling out any employee
D. ask one of your employees to discuss the matter with the individual

17. One of your employees submitted an application for acceptance into a career development workshop two months ago and has heard nothing. The individual tells you that when one of her co-workers submitted an application, he received a reply a week later. 17.____
Which is the BEST response for you to make?
A. This is obviously a case of discrimination. I'll bring it to the Affirmative Action officer immediately.
B. Next time you submit a request for something of this nature, let me know and I will write a cover letter that will carry more weight.
C. Perhaps it was an oversight. Why don't you call the organization and ask why you've heard nothing?
D. it looks like you won't be accepted this year. Be sure to try again next year.

18. In order to meet deadlines, a supervisor should 18.____
    A. schedule the work and keep informed of its progress
    B. delegate work
    C. hire temporary personnel
    D. know the capabilities of his or her most reliable employees

19. Your supervisor has given instructions to your employees in your absence that differ from those you had given them. 19.____
    You should
    A. have your employees follow your instructions
    B. have your employees follow your supervisor's instructions
    C. discuss the matter with your supervisor
    D. discuss the matter with your employees and find out which method they think is best

20. You have found it necessary to return an assignment completed by one of your employees so that several changes can be made. The employee objects to making these changes. 20.____
    The MOST appropriate action for you to take FIRST is to
    A. inform the employee that he or she is free to object to your supervisor
    B. ask if the employee has carefully read your proposed changes
    C. calmly state that your decision is final, and further discussion will most likely be useless
    D. allow the employee to present his or her objections against making the changes

21. Among the problems that confront a new supervisor in relation to her or his employees, the one which requires the MOST unusual degree of skill and diplomacy is 21.____
    A. changing established ideas
    B. calling attention to mistakes
    C. gaining the respect of employees
    D. training new employees

22. Of the following, the BEST indication of high morale in a supervisor's unit would be the 22.____
    A. unit never has to work overtime
    B. supervisor often enjoys staying late to plan work for the following day
    C. unit gives expensive birthday presents to each other
    D. employees are willing to give first priority to attaining group objectives, subordinating personal desires they may have

23. In the satisfactory handling of an employee's complaint which is fancied rather than real, the complaint should be considered 23.____
    A. not very important since it has no basis in fact
    B. as important as a grievance grounded in fact
    C. an attempt by the employee to create trouble
    D. an indication of a psychological problem on the part of the employee

24. You are attempting to teach a new employee in your unit how to change a typewriter ribbon. The employee is having a great deal of difficulty changing the ribbon, even though you have always found it simple to do. 24.____
Before you spend more time instructing the individual, you should
   A. ask if the employee working nearest would take responsibility for changing the ribbon in the future
   B. tell the employee that you never found this difficult and ask what he or she finds difficult about it
   C. review each of the steps you have already explained and determine whether the individual understands them
   D. tell the employee that you will continue after lunch because you are getting irritable

25. One of your workers has relatives who raise chickens. One day, you mention in casual conversation that you bought some eggs of poor quality at the grocery store. The following Monday, the worker places a box of fresh eggs on your desk. You thank him and offer to pay, but he refuses. On several occasions thereafter, he brings in additional eggs but still refuses to take payment. He is obviously proud of these products and seems to take great pleasure in sharing them with you. However, you begin to hear rumors that the other workers believe that you and the worker are very friendly and that he is receiving special privileges from you. 25.____
You should
   A. explain the situation to the worker, pointing out that he is being hurt by the conditions because of the feelings of others
   B. ignore the situation since the worker is merely being friendly and is actually receiving no favors in return
   C. supervise this worker more carefully than the others to insure that he will not take advantage of the situation
   D. refuse all gifts from the worker thereafter without further explanation

KEY (CORRECT ANSWERS)

1. C
2. D
3. B
4. D
5. A

6. D
7. B
8. B
9. A
10. B

11. C
12. D
13. C
14. C
15. B

16. B
17. C
18. A
19. C
20. D

21. A
22. D
23. B
24. C
25. A

TEST 4

DIRECTIONS: Each question or incomplete statement is followed by several suggested answers or completions. Select the one that BEST answers the question or completes the statement. *PRINT THE LETTER OF THE CORRECT ANSWER IN THE SPACE AT THE RIGHT.*

1. Lax supervision has been blamed largely on the unwillingness of supervisors to supervise their employees. 1.____
The CHIEF reason for this unwillingness to supervise is based MAINLY on the supervisors'
   A. failure to accept modern concepts of proper supervision
   B. doubt of their ability to keep pace with modern techniques and developments in supervision
   C. fear of complaints from employees and the supervisors' wish to avoid unpleasantness
   D. inability to adhere to the same high standards of performance which are required of employees

2. The appraisal of employees and their performance is an integral part of the supervisor's job. There is wide agreement that several basic principles must be taken into account by supervisors involved in the appraisal process in order to perform this function correctly. 2.____
The one of the statements below that LEAST represents a basic principle of the appraisal process is:
   A. Appraisals should be based more on performance of definite tasks than on personality considerations.
   B. Appraisal of long-range potential should rely heavily on subjective judgment of that potential.
   C. Appraisal involves the use of value judgments by the supervisor and does, therefore, require reference to pre-established standards.
   D. Appraisal should aim at emphasizing employees' strengths rather than weaknesses.

3. Although accuracy and speed are both important in the performance of work, accuracy should be considered more important MAINLY because 3.____
   A. most supervisors insist on accurate work
   B. much time is lost in correcting errors
   C. a rapid rate of work cannot be maintained for any length of time
   D. speedy workers are often inaccurate

4. If an employee has done a complicated task well, his or her supervisor should 4.____
   A. tell the employee that he or she has done a good job
   B. call a staff meeting to see if anyone has suggestions for improving future performance of the task
   C. avoid commending the employee as performing competently is what they are paid to do
   D. confide in the employee that he or she is the best worker in your unit

5. You are a newly appointed supervisor in a large office. It had been the practice in that office for the employees to take an unauthorized coffee break at 10:00 A.M. You have been successful in stopping this practice, and for one week no one had gone out for coffee at 10:00 A.M. One day, a stenographer comes over to you at 10:15 A.M., appearing to be ill. She states that she doesn't feel well and that she would like to go out for a cup of tea. She asks your permission to leave the office for a few minutes. 5.____
You should
   A. telephone and have a cup of tea delivered to her
   B. permit her to go out
   C. refuse her permission, explaining that you don't wish to set a bad example
   D. tell her she can leave for an early lunch

6. One of the employees you supervise has just put up a small poster in her work area that two of your eight employees find obscene and distasteful. While you don't like the poster either, it doesn't upset you. The two employees already have complained to you about the poster. 6.____
Of the following, you should
   A. have the two employees talk to the individual and explain why they are offended
   B. privately explain to the individual that her poster is causing some problems and seek her cooperation in removing it
   C. do nothing as the employee has the right to express her feelings
   D. compromise and allow her to display the poster half of the time

7. One of the most effective ways to build a sense of employee pride, teamwork, and motivation is for the supervisor to seek advice, suggestions, and information from employees concerning ways in which work should be solved. Many experiments in group decision-making have indicated that work groups can help the supervisor in improving decision-making. Where employees feel that they are really part of a team and that they have a significant influence on the decisions that are made, they are more likely to accept the decisions and to seek new solutions to future difficult problems. 7.____
According to the above passage, a supervisor should
   A. almost always follow the advice of his or her employees in handling difficult problems
   B. always seek advice from employees when handling difficult problems
   C. choices A and D, but not B
   D. look to employees for assistance in decision-making

8. You have just had a private discussion with the employee with the poster in Question 6 above. You have explained that her poster is causing some problems, and have asked for her cooperation in removing it. She has politely refused to do so, saying, "looking at it cheers her up, and she's been depressed lately." 8.____
You should
   A. wait a day or two to see if the incident blows over before deciding whether to take any further action

B. call in the two disgruntled employees within the hour and let them know they'll have to live with the poster as you are not going to act as a censor in the office
C. check agency policies to see if it is legal to have posters down as it is interfering with the work of the unit

9. An employee reprimanded for poor performance tells her supervisor that her recent behavior has been due to a serious family problem. The supervisor suggests several programs which may be able to help her. 9.____
The action of the supervisor was
A. *inappropriate*; the supervisor should not involve herself in the personal affairs of her subordinates
B. *appropriate*; personal problems frequently affect job performance
C. *inappropriate*; the employee may consider the supervisor responsible for the subsequent action of the social agencies
D. *appropriate*; the discussion with the supervisor will in itself tend to solve the problem

10. Your supervisor informs you that the employee turnover rate in your office is well above the norm and must be reduced. 10.____
Which one of the following initial steps would be LEAST appropriate in attempting to overcome this problem?
A. Decide to be more lenient about the performance standards and about employee requests for time off, so that your office will gain a reputation as a good place to work.
B. Discuss the problem with a few of your employees whose judgment you trust to see if they can provide insight into the underlying causes of the problem.
C. Review the records of employees who have left during the past year to see if they can shed some light on the underlying causes of the problem.
D. Carefully review your training procedures to see if they can be improved

11. The management principle that each employee should be under the direct control of one immediate supervisor at any one time is known as the principle of 11.____
A. chain of command
B. span of control
C. unity of command
D. homogeneous assignment

12. The employees of a unit have been wasteful in the use of office supplies. 12.____
Of the following, the MOST desirable action for the supervisor to take to reduce this waste is to
A. determine the average quantity of supplies used daily by each employee
B. find out which employees have been most wasteful and reprimand those employees
C. discuss this matter at a conference with the staff, pointing out the necessity for, and methods of, eliminating waste
D. issue supplies for an assignment at the time the assignment is made and limit the quantity to the amount needed for that assignment only

13. You supervise nineteen employees in a unit which is located directly across from the commissioner's office. One of your new employees has a habit of *showing off* whenever the commissioner is nearby. You have just heard other employees laughing about this behavior among themselves. You like the new employee and would like the employee to be accepted by the others. 13.____
Of the following, you should
   A. discuss the situation with two of the older employees and seek their cooperation in being a little more tolerant
   B. talk with the new employee and gently explain the situation
   C. discuss the situation with your most trusted employees and ask them to talk to the others
   D. do nothing

14. One of your employees comes to you and complains of sexual harassment by your supervisor. The employee has frequently complained about minor issues in the six months she's been there. You have known your supervisor for thirteen years and respect him a great deal. You have known your supervisor for thirteen years and respect him a great deal. 14.____
Of the following, you should
   A. firmly let the employee know what a serious allegation she is bringing against your supervisor
   B. let the employee know you will take her concerns seriously
   C. call your supervisor and give him a chance to prepare a defense
   D. inform the employee that she had better have concrete proof for a charge of this nature

15. The one of the following which is usually the POOREST reason for transferring an employee is to 15.____
   A. grant a doctor's request that the employee work nearer to his or her home
   B. take care of changes in workload
   C. relieve the monotony of work assignments

16. You find that you have unjustly reprimanded one of your subordinates. 16.____
You should
   A. ignore the matter, but be more careful in the future
   B. readily admit your mistake to the employee
   C. admit your mistake at your next staff meeting so that your employees will know how fair you are
   D. admit your mistake, but blame the misunderstanding on your supervisor

17. An experienced, self-confident employee carelessly omitted an essential operation on a job assigned to her. As a result, the completion of an important urgent report was delayed for several hours. A few days later, a relatively inexperienced, sensitive co-worker made a similar careless mistake with similar negative results. The supervisor of the two employees was more gentle in reprimanding the latter than the former employee. 17.____

The supervisor's action in administering reprimands of unequal severity to these two subordinates was

A. *not appropriate*, because fairness requires that subordinates responsible for like mistakes receive reprimands of like severity
B. *appropriate*, because supervisors should consider the temperament of subordinates when reprimanding them
C. *appropriate*, because subordinates who accept greater responsibilities must likewise accept the consequent greater penalties for their mistakes
D. *not appropriate*, because more experienced employees benefit less, in general, from reprimands than less experienced employees

18. You have just overheard a tense discussion in the cafeteria between two of your best employees. One of them has owed the other $40 for several months and has not paid it back or even mentioned the debt. The employees do not realize that you have heard them. 18.____
During that week, you should
A. not discuss the matter with either of them
B. discuss the matter with both of them, as the conflict may adversely affect their job performance
C. discuss the matter with the one who has not paid back the money
D. put a clever but meaningful cartoon up on your wall about the importance of paying back debts to friends

19. You have been supervising twenty employees for three months. You suspect that one of your employees, who has worked in the unit longer than anyone else, has perfected the art of looking busy. You wish to find out how much work she is really accomplishing. 19.____
Of the following, it would be LEAST appropriate to
A. have a frank discussion with the employee about her performance
B. set specific time limits on when you would like to get work back from her
C. try to observe her more carefully while she is working
D. be more careful when monitoring her work output

20. The supervisor of a central files bureau which has fifty employees customarily spends a considerable portion of time in spot-checking the files, reviewing material being transferred from active to inactive files, and similar activities. 20.____
From the viewpoint of the department management, the MOST pertinent evaluation which can be made on the basis of this information is that the
A. supervisor is conscientious and hardworking
B. bureau may need additional staff
C. supervisor has not made a sufficient delegation of authority and responsibility
D. bureau needs an in-service training course as the work of its employees requires an abnormal amount of review

21. You have just been appointed as supervisor of ten employees. The supervisor you are replacing demanded that her subordinate accept their assignments without question. She refused to allow them to exercise initiative in carrying out assignments and maintained a constant check on their work performance. 21.____

The MOST appropriate policy for you to adopt would be to
A. gradually remove the controls you consider too strict and provide opportunities for your staff to participate in formulating work plans and procedures
B. continue her rigid policies, as the employees are used to this
C. discontinue all strict controls immediately and give the employees complete freedom in carrying out their assignments
D. ask your employees what method of supervision they would prefer

22. In any agency, the top administrative officials are concerned largely with the work of overall creative planning with respect to the anticipated progress of the agency. The first-line supervisors, on the other hand, are concerned largely with the control of current action for the execution of current jobs. 22.____
On the basis of this quotation, a first-line supervisor would be CHIEFLY responsible for
A. increasing or decreasing the responsibilities of his or her unit to reflect changes in the policies of the agency
B. modifying the work assignments of his or her present staff to handle a seasonal variation in the activities of the unit
C. revising the procedure that is used for transmitting instructions from the head of the agency to the unit heads
D. raising and lowering the production goals of his or her unit as often as necessary to adjust them to the abilities of employees

23. As a supervisor, you may find it necessary to consult with your superior before taking action on some matters. 23.____
Of the following, the action for which it is MOST important that you obtain the prior approval of your superior is one that involves
A. assuming additional functions for your unit
B. rotating assignments among your staff members
C. initiating regular meetings of your staff
D. assigning certain members of your staff to work overtime on an emergency job

24. Suppose that a clerk who is employed in a unit under your supervision performs his work quickly but carelessly. He is about to be transferred to another unit in your department. The chief of this other unit asks you for your opinion of this employee's work habits. The chief of this other unit asks you for your opinion of this employee's work habits. 24.____
Of the following, the MOST appropriate reply for you to make is to
A. point out this employee's good qualities only since he may correct his bad qualities after his transfer is effected
B. say nothing good or bad about this employee, thus permitting him to start his new assignment with a clean slate
C. inform the unit chief that this clerk performed his work speedily but was careless
D. emphasize his employee's good points and minimize his bad points

25. Of the following, the action that is likely to contribute MOST to the prestige of a supervisor is for him to 25.____
    A. expect al his subordinates to perform with equal efficiency any tasks assigned to them
    B. observe the same rules of conduct that he expects his subordinates to observe
    C. seek their advice on his personal problems and offer them his advice on their personal problems
    D. be always frank and outspoken to his subordinates in pointing out their faults

KEY (CORRECT ANSWERS)

1. C
2. B
3. B
4. A
5. B

6. B
7. D
8. A
9. B
10. A

11. C
12. C
13. D
14. B
15. D

16. B
17. B
18. A
19. A
20. C

21. A
22. B
23. A
24. C
25. C

NAME AND NUMBER CHECKING

EXAMINATION SECTION

TEST 1

DIRECTIONS: This test is designed to measure your speed/and accuracy. You are urged to work both quickly and accurately and to do correctly as many lists as you can in the time allowed. The test consists of lists or pairs of names and numbers. Count the number of IDENTICAL pairs in each list. Then, select the correct number, 1, 2, 3, 4, 5, and indicate your choice in the space at the right. Two sample questions are presented for your guidance, together with the correct solutions.

SAMPLE LIST A
Adelphi College – Adelphia College
Braxton Corp – Braxeton Corp.
Wassaic State School – Wassaic State School
Central Islip State Hospital – Central Isllip State Hospital
Greenwich House – Greenwich House

NOTE: There are only two correct pairs—Wassaic State School and Greenwich House. Therefore, the CORRECT answer is 2.

SAMPLE LIST B
78453694 – 78453684
784530 – 784530
533 – 534
67845 – 67845
2368745 – 2368755

NOTE: There are only two correct pairs—784530 and 67845. Therefore, the CORRECT answer is 2.

LIST 1 1.____

Diagnostic Clinic	– Diagnostic Clinic
Yorkville Health	– Yorkville Health
Meinhard Clinic	– Meinhart Clinic
Corlears Clinic	– Carlears Clinic
Tremont Diagnostic	– Tremont Diagnostic

LIST 2 2.____

73526	– 73526
7283627198	– 7283627198
627	– 637
728352617283	– 7283526178282
6281	– 6281

LIST 3		3.____
Jefferson Clinic	– Jeffersen Clinic	
Mott Haven Center	– Mott Havan Center	
Bronx Hospital	– Bronx Hospital	
Montefiore Hospital	– Montifeore Hospital	
Beth Isreal Hospital	– Beth Israel Hospital	
LIST 4		4.____
936271826	– 936371826	
5271	– 5291	
82637192037	– 82637192037	
527182	– 5271882	
726354256	- 72635456	
LIST 5		5.____
Trinity Hospital	– Trinity Hospital	
Central Harlem	– Centrel Harlem	
St. Luke's Hospital	– St. Lukes' Hospital	
Mt. Sinai Hospital	– Mt. Sinia Hospital	
N.Y. Dispensery	– N.Y. Dispensary	
LIST 6		6.____
725361552637	– 725361555637	
7526378	– 7526377	
6975	– 6975	
82637481028	– 82637481028	
3427	– 3429	
LIST 7		7.____
Misericordia Hospital	– Miseracordia Hospital	
Lebonan Hospital	– Lebanon Hospital	
Gouverneur Hospital	– Gouverner Hospital	
German Polyclinic	– German Policlinic	
French Hospital	– French Hospital	
LIST 8		8.____
8277364933251	– 827364933351	
63728	– 63728	
367281	– 367281	
62733846273	– 6273846293	
62836	- 6283	
LIST 9		9.____
King's County Hospital	– Kings County Hospital	
St. Johns Long Island	– St. John's Long Island	
Bellevue Hospital	– Bellvue Hospital	
Beth David Hospital	– Beth David Hospital	
Samaritan Hospital	– Samariton Hospital	

LIST 10 10.____

62836454	– 62836455
42738267	– 42738369
573829	– 573829
738291627874	– 738291627874
725	- 735

LIST 11 11.____

Bloomingdal Clinic	– Bloomingdale Clinic
Communitty Hospital	– Community Hospital
Metroplitan Hospital	– Metropoliton Hospital
Lenox Hill Hospital	– Lonex Hill Hospital
Lincoln Hospital	– Lincoln Hospital

LIST 12 12.____

6283364728	– 6283648
627385	– 627383
54283902	– 54283602
63354	– 63354
7283562781	- 7283562781

LIST 13 13.____

Sydenham Hospital	– Sydanham Hospital
Roosevalt Hospital	– Roosevelt Hospital
Vanderbilt Clinic	– Vanderbild Clinic
Women's Hospital	– Woman's Hospital
Flushing Hospital	– Flushing Hospital

LIST 14 14.____

62738	– 62738
727355542321	– 72735542321
263849332	– 263849332
262837	– 263837
47382912	- 47382922

LIST 15 15.____

Episcopal Hospital	– Episcapal Hospital
Flower Hospital	– Flouer Hospital
Stuyvesent Clinic	– Stuyvesant Clinic
Jamaica Clinic	– Jamaica Clinic
Ridgwood Clinic	– Ridgewood Clinic

LIST 16 16.____

628367299	– 628367399
111	– 111
118293304829	– 1182839489
4448	– 4448
333693678	- 333693678

LIST 17 17.____

Arietta Crane Farm	– Areitta Crane Farm	
Bikur Chilim Home	– Bikur Chilom Home	
Burke Foundation	– Burke Foundation	
Blythedale Home	– Blythdale Home	
Campbell Cottages	– Cambell Cottages	

LIST 18 18.____

32123	– 32132
273893326783	– 27389326783
473829	– 473829
7382937	– 7383937
3628890122332	- 36289012332

LIST 19 19.____

Caraline Rest	– Caroline Rest
Loreto Rest	– Loretto Rest
Edgewater Creche	– Edgwater Creche
Holiday Farm	– Holiday Farm
House of St. Giles	– House of st. Giles

LIST 20 20.____

557286777	– 55728677
3678902	– 3678892
1567839	– 1567839
7865434712	– 7865344712
9927382	- 9927382

LIST 21 21.____

Isabella Home	– Isabela Home
James A. Moore Home	– James A. More Home
The Robin's Nest	– The Roben's Nest
Pelham Home	– Pelam Home
St. Eleanora's Home	– St. Eleanora's Home

LIST 22 22.____

273648293048	– 273648293048
334	– 334
7362536478	– 7362536478
7362819273	– 7362819273
7362	- 7363

LIST 23 23.____

St. Pheobe's Mission	– St. Phebe's Mission
Seaside Home	– Seaside Home
Speedwell Society	– Speedwell Society
Valeria Home	– Valera Home
Wiltwyck	- Wildwyck

LIST 24 | 24.____

63728	– 63738	
63728192736	– 63728192738	
428	– 458	
62738291527	– 62738291529	
63728192	- 63728192	

LIST 25 | 25.____

McGaffin	– McGafin	
David Ardslee	– David Ardslee	
Axton Supply	– Axeton Supply Co	
Alice Russell	– Alice Russell	
Dobson Mfg. Co.	– Dobsen Mfg. Co.	

KEY (CORRECT ANSWERS)

1.	3	11.	1
2.	3	12.	2
3.	1	13.	1
4.	1	14.	2
5.	1	15.	1
6.	2	16.	3
7.	1	17.	1
8.	2	18.	1
9.	1	19.	1
10.	2	20.	2

21.	1
22.	4
23.	2
24.	1
25.	2

TEST 2

DIRECTIONS: This test is designed to measure your speed/and accuracy. You are urged to work both quickly and accurately and to do correctly as many lists as you can in the time allowed. The test consists of lists or pairs of names and numbers. Count the number of IDENTICAL pairs in each list. Then, select the correct number, 1, 2, 3, 4, 5, and indicate your choice in the space at the right.

LIST 1 — 1.____

82637381028	– 82637281028
928	– 928
72937281028	– 72937281028
7362	– 7362
927382615	– 927382615

LIST 2 — 2.____

Albee Theatre	– Albee Theatre
Lapland Lumber Co.	– Laplund Lumber Co.
Adelphi College	– Adelphi College
Jones & Son Inc.	– Jones & Sons Inc.
S.W. Ponds Co.	– S.W. Ponds Co.

LIST 3 — 3.____

85345	– 85345
895643278	– 895643277
726352	– 726353
632685	– 632685
7263524	– 7236524

LIST 4 — 4.____

Eagle Library	– Eagle Library
Dodge Ltd.	– Dodge Co.
Stromberg Carlson	– Stromberg Carlsen
Clairice Ling	– Clairice Linng
Mason Book Co.	– Matson Book Co.

LIST 5 — 5.____

66273	– 66273
629	– 629
7382517283	– 7382517283
637281	– 639281
2738261	– 2788261

LIST 6 — 6.____

Robert MacColl	– Robert McColl
Buick Motor	– Buck Motors
Murray Bay & Co. Ltd.	– Murray Bay Co. Ltd.
L.T. Ltyle	– L.T. Lyttle
A.S. Landas	– A.S. Landas

LIST 7 7.____

6271526374890	– 627152637490
73526189	– 73526189
5372	– 5392
637281142	– 63728124
4783946	– 4783046

LIST 8 8.____

Tyndall Burke	– Tyndell Burke
W. Briehl	– W. Briehl
Burritt Publishing Co.	– Buritt Publishing Co.
Frederick Breyer & Co.	– Frederick Breyer Co.
Bailey Buulard	– Bailey Bullard

LIST 9 9.____

634	– 634
16837	– 163837
273892223678	– 27389223678
527182	– 527782
3628901223	– 3629002223

LIST 10 10.____

Ernest Boas	– Ernest Boas
Rankin Barne	– Rankin Barnes
Edward Appley	– Edward Appely
Camel	– Camel
Caiger Food Co.	– Caiger Food Co.

LIST 11 11.____

6273	– 6273
322	– 332
15672839	– 15672839
63728192637	– 63728192639
738	– 738

LIST 12 12.____

Wells Fargo Co.	– Wells Fargo Co.
W.D. Brett	– W.D. Britt
Tassco Co.	– Tassko Co.
Republic Mills	– Republic Mill
R.W. Burnham	– R.W. Burhnam

LIST 13 13.____

7253529152	– 7283529152
6283	– 6383
52839102738	– 5283910238
308	– 398
82637201927	– 8263720127

LIST 14		14.____
Schumacker Co.	– Shumacker Co.	
C.H. Caiger	– C.H. Caiger	
Abraham Strauss	– Abram Straus	
B.F. Boettjer	– B.F. Boettijer	
Cut-Rate Store	– Cut-Rate Stores	
LIST 15		15.____
15273826	– 15273826	
72537	– 73537	
726391027384	– 62639107384	
637389	– 627399	
725382910	– 725382910	
LIST 16		16.____
Hixby Ltd.	– Hixby Lt'd.	
S. Reiner	– S. Riener	
Reynard Co.	– Reynord Co.	
Esso Gassoline Co.	– Esso Gasolene Co.	
Belle Brock	– Belle Brock	
LIST 17		17.____
7245	– 7245	
819263728192	– 819263728172	
682537289	– 682537298	
789	– 789	
82936542891	– 82936542891	
LIST 18		18.____
Joseph Cartwright	– Joseph Cartwrite	
Foote Food Co.	– Foot Food Co.	
Weiman & Held	– Weiman & Held	
Sanderson Shoe Co.	– Sandersen Shoe Co.	
A.M. Byrne	– A.N. Byrne	
LIST 19		19.____
4738267	– 4738277	
63728	– 63729	
6283628901	– 6283628991	
918264	– 918264	
263728192037	– 2637728192073	
LIST 20		20.____
Exray Laboratories	– Exray Labratories	
Curley Toy Co.	– Curly Toy Co.	
J. Lauer & Cross	– J. Laeur & Cross	
Mireco Brands	– Mireco Brands	
Sandor Lorand	– Sandor Larand	

LIST 21		21.____
607	– 609	
6405	– 6403	
976	– 996	
101267	– 101267	
2065432	– 20965432	
LIST 22		22.____
John Macy & Sons	– John Macy & Son	
Venus Pencil Co.	– Venus Pencil Co.	
Nell McGinnis	– Nell McGinnis	
McCutcheon & Co.	– McCutcheon & Co.	
Sun-Tan Oil	– Sun-Tan Oil	
LIST 23		23.____
703345700	– 703345700	
46754	– 466754	
3367490	– 3367490	
3379	– 3778	
47384	– 47394	
LIST 24		24.____
arthritis	– arthritis	
asthma	– asthma	
endocrine	– endocrene	
gastro-enterological	– gastrol-enteralogical	
orthopedic	– orthopedic	
LIST 25		25.____
743829432	– 743828432	
998	– 998	
732816253902	– 732816252902	
46829	– 46830	
7439120249	– 7439210249	

KEY (CORRECT ANSWERS)

1.	4
2.	3
3.	2
4.	1
5.	2
6.	1
7.	2
8.	1
9.	1
10.	3
11.	3
12.	1
13.	1
14.	1
15.	2
16.	1
17.	3
18.	1
19.	1
20.	1
21.	1
22.	4
23.	2
24.	3
25.	1

CLERICAL ABILITIES

EXAMINATION SECTION

TEST 1

DIRECTIONS: Each question or incomplete statement is followed by several suggested answers or completions. Select the one that BEST answers the question or completes the statement. *PRINT THE LETTER OF THE CORRECT ANSWER IN THE SPACE AT THE RIGHT.*

Questions 1-4.

DIRECTIONS: Questions 1 through 4 are to be answered on the basis of the information given below.

The most commonly used filing system and the one that is easiest to learn is alphabetical filing. This involves putting records in an A to Z order, according to the letters of the alphabet. The name of a person is filed by using the following order: first, the surname or last name; second, the first name; third, the middle name or middle initial. For example, *Henry C. Young* is filed under *Y* and thereafter under *Young, Henry C.* The name of a company is filed in the same way. For example, *Long Cabinet Co.* is filed under *L* while *John T. Long Cabinet Co.* is filed under *L* and thereafter under *Long, John T. Cabinet Co.*

1. The one of the following which lists the names of persons in the CORRECT alphabetical order is: 1.____
   A. Mary Carrie, Helen Carrol, James Carson, John Carter
   B. James Carson, Mary Carrie, John Carter, Helen Carrol
   C. Helen Carrol, James Carson, John Carter, Mary Carrie
   D. John Carter, Helen Carrol, Mary Carrie, James Carson

2. The one of the following which lists the names of persons in the CORRECT alphabetical order is: 2.____
   A. Jones, John C.; Jones, John A.; Jones, John P.; Jones, John K.
   B. Jones, John P.; Jones, John K.; Jones, John C.; Jones, John A.
   C. Jones, John A.; Jones, John C.; Jones, John K.; Jones, John P.
   D. Jones, John K.; Jones, John C.; Jones, John A.; Jones, John P.

3. The one of the following which lists the names of the companies in the CORRECT alphabetical order is: 3.____
   A. Blane Co., Blake Co., Block Co., Blear Co.
   B. Blake Co., Blane Co., Blear Co., Block Co.
   C. Block Co., Blear Co., Blane Co., Blake Co.
   D. Blear Co., Blake Co., Blane Co., Block Co.

4. You are to return to the file an index card on *Barry C. Wayne Materials and Supplies Co.* 4.____
Of the following, the CORRECT alphabetical group that you should return the index card to is
A. A to G B. H to M C. N to S D. T to Z

Questions 5-10.

DIRECTIONS: In each of Questions 5 through 10, the names of four people are given. For each question, choose as your answer the one of the four names given which should be filed FIRST according to the usual system of alphabetical filing of names, as described in the following paragraph.

In filing names, you must start with the last name. Names are filed in order of the first letter of the last name, then the second letter, etc. Therefore, BAILY would be filed before BROWN, which would be filed before COLT. A name with fewer letters of the same type comes first, i.e., Smith before Smithe. If the last names are the same, the names are filed alphabetically by the first name. If the first name is an initial, a name with an initial would come before a first name that starts with the same letter as the initial. Therefore, I. BROWN would come before IRA BROWN. Finally, if both last name and first name are the same, the name would be filed alphabetically by the middle name, once again an initial coming before a middle name which starts with the same letter as the initial. If there is no middle name at all, the name would come before those with middle initials or names.

SAMPLE QUESTION:
A. Lester Daniels
B. William Dancer
C. Nathan Danzig
D. Dan Lester

The last names beginning with D are filed before the last name beginning with L. Since DANIELS, DANCER, and DANZIG all begin with the same three letters, you must look at the fourth letter of the last name to determine which name should be filed first. C comes before I or Z in the alphabet, so DANCER is filed before DANIELS or DANZIG. Therefore, the answer to the above sample question is B.

5. A. Scott Biala 5.____
B. Mary Byala
C. Martin Baylor
D. Francis Bauer

6. A. Howard J. Black 6.____
B. Howard Black
C. J. Howard Black
D. John H. Black

7. A. Theodora Garth Kingston 7.____
B. Theadore Barth Kingston
C. Thomas Kingston
D. Thomas T. Kingston

8. A. Paulette Mary Huerta 8.____
   B. Paul M. Huerta
   C. Paulette L. Huerta
   D. Peter A. Huerta

9. A. Martha Hunt Morgan 9.____
   B. Martin Hunt Morgan
   C. Mary H. Morgan
   D. Martine H. Morgan

10. A. James T. Meerschaum 10.____
    B. James M. Mershum
    C. James F. Mearshaum
    D. James N. Meshum

Questions 11-14.

DIRECTIONS: Questions 11 through 14 are to be answered SOLELY on the basis of the following information.

You are required to file various documents in file drawers which are labeled according to the following pattern:

DOCUMENTS

MEMOS		LETTERS	
File	Subject	File	Subject
84PM1	(A-L)	84PC1	(A-L)
84PM2	(M-Z)	84PC2	(M-Z)

REPORTS		INQUIRIES	
File	Subject	File	Subject
84PR1	(A-L)	84PQ1	(A-L)
84PR2	(M-Z)	84PQ2	(M-Z)

11. A letter dealing with a burglary should be filed in the drawer labeled 11.____
    A. 84PM1 B. 84PC1 C. 84PR1 D. 84PQ2

12. A report on Statistics should be found in the drawer labeled 12.____
    A. 84PM1 B. 84PC2 C. 84PR2 D. 84PQS

13. An inquiry is received about parade permit procedures. It should be filed in the drawer labeled 13.____
    A. 84PM2 B. 84PC1 C. 84PR1 D. 84PQ2

14. A police officer has a question about a robbery report you filed. You should pull this file from the drawer labeled 14.____
    A. 84PM1 B. 84PM2 C. 84PR1 D. 84PR2

Questions 15-22.

DIRECTIONS: Each of Questions 15 through 22 consists of four or six numbered names. For each question, choose the option (A, B, C, or D) which indicates the order in which the names should be filed in accordance with the following filing instructions:

- File alphabetically according to last name, then first name, then middle initial.
- File according to each successive letter within a name.
- When comparing two names in which the letters in the longer name are identical to the corresponding letters in the shorter name, the shorter name is filed first.
- When the last names are the same, initials are always filed before names beginning with the same letter.

15. I. Ralph Robinson 15.____
II. Alfred Ross
III. Luis Robles
IV. James Roberts

The CORRECT filing sequence for the above names should be
A. IV, II, I, III B. I, IV, III, II C. III, IV, I, II D. IV, I, III, II

16. I. Irwin Goodwin 16.____
II. Inez Gonzalez
III. Irene Goodman
IV. Ira S. Goodwin
V. Ruth I. Goldstein
VI. M.B. Goodman

The CORRECT filing sequence for the above names should be
A. V, II, I, IV, III, VI
B. V, II, VI, III, IV, I
C. V, II, III, VI, IV, I
D. V, II, III, VI, I, IV

17. I. George Allan 17.____
II. Gregory Allen
III. Gary Allen
IV. George Allen

The CORRECT filing sequence for the above names should be
A. IV, III, I, II B. I, IV, II, III C. III, IV, I, II D. I, III, IV, II

18. I. Simon Kauffman 18.____
 II. Leo Kaufman
 III. Robert Kaufmann
 IV. Paul Kauffmann

 The CORRECT filing sequence for the above names should be
 A. I, IV, II, III B. II, IV, III, I C. III, II, IV, I D. I, II, III, IV

19. I. Roberta Williams 19.____
 II. Robin Wilson
 III. Roberta Wilson
 IV. Robin Williams

 The CORRECT filing sequence for the above names should be
 A. III, II, IV, I B. I, IV, III, II C. I, II, III, IV D. III, I, II, IV

20. I. Lawrence Shultz 20.____
 II. Albert Schultz
 III. Theodore Schwartz
 IV. Thomas Schwarz
 V. Alvin Schultz
 VI. Leonard Shultz

 The CORRECT filing sequence for the above names should be
 A. II, V, III, IV, I, VI B. IV, III, V, I, II, VI
 C. II, V, I, VI, III, IV D. I, VI, II, V, III, IV

21. I. McArdle 21.____
 II. Mayer
 III. Maletz
 IV. McNiff
 V. Meyer
 VI. MacMahon

 The CORRECT filing sequence for the above names should be
 A. I, IV, VI, III, II, V B. II, I, IV, VI, III, V
 C. VI, III, II, I, IV, V D. VI, III, II, V, I, IV

22. I. Jack E. Johnson 22.____
 II. R.H. Jackson
 III. Bertha Jackson
 IV. J.T. Johnson
 V. Ann Johns
 VI. John Jacobs

 The CORRECT filing sequence for the above names should be
 A. II, III, VI, V, IV, I B. III, II, VI, V, IV, I
 C. VI, II, III, I, V, IV D. III, II, VI, IV, V, I

Questions 23-30.

DIRECTIONS: The code table below shows 10 letters with matching numbers. For each question, there are three sets of letters. Each set of letters is followed by a set of numbers which may or may not match their correct letter according to the code table. For each question, check all three sets of letters and numbers and mark your answer:

A. if no pairs are correctly matched
B. if only one pair is correctly matched
C. if only two pairs are correctly matched
D. if all three pairs are correctly matched

CODE TABLE

T	M	V	D	S	P	R	G	B	H
1	2	3	4	5	6	7	8	9	0

SAMPLE QUESTION: TMVDSP – 123456
RGBHTM – 789011
DSPRGB – 256789

In the sample question above, the first set of numbers correctly match its set of letters. But the second and third pairs contain mistakes. In the second pair, M is correctly matched with number 1. According to the code table, letter M should be correctly matched with number 2. In the third pair, the letter D is incorrectly matched with number 2. According to the code table, letter D should be correctly matched with number 4. Since only one of the pairs is correctly matched, the answer to this sample question is B.

23. RSBMRM – 759262 23.____
GDSRVH – 845730
VDBRTM - 349713

24. TGVSDR – 183247 24.____
SMHRDP – 520647
TRMHSR - 172057

25. DSPRGM – 456782 25.____
MVDBHT – 234902
HPMDBT - 062491

26. BVPTRD – 936184 26.____
GDPHMB – 807029
GMRHMV - 827032

27. MGVRSH – 283750 27.____
TRDMBS – 174295
SPRMGV - 567283

28. SGBSDM – 489542 28.____
MGHPTM – 290612
MPBMHT - 269301

29. TDPBHM – 146902 29.____
VPBMRS – 369275
GDMBHM - 842902

30. MVPTBV – 236194 30.____
PDRTMB – 47128
BGTMSM - 981232

KEY (CORRECT ANSWERS)

1.	A	11.	B	21.	C
2.	C	12.	C	22.	B
3.	B	13.	D	23.	B
4.	D	14.	D	24.	B
5.	D	15.	D	25.	C
6.	B	16.	C	26.	A
7.	B	17.	D	27.	D
8.	B	18.	A	28.	A
9.	A	19.	B	29.	D
10.	C	20.	A	30.	A

TEST 2

DIRECTIONS: Each question or incomplete statement is followed by several suggested answers or completions. Select the one that BEST answers the question or completes the statement. *PRINT THE LETTER OF THE CORRECT ANSWER IN THE SPACE AT THE RIGHT.*

Questions 1-10.

DIRECTIONS: Questions 1 through 10 each consists of two columns, each containing four lines of names, numbers and/or addresses. For each question, compare the lines in Column I with the lines in Column II to see if they match exactly, and mark your answer A, B, C, or D, according to the following instructions:

A. all four lines match exactly
B. only three lines match exactly
C. only two lines match exactly
D. only one line matches exactly

		COLUMN I	COLUMN II	
1.	I.	Earl Hodgson	Earl Hodgson	1.____
	II.	1409870	1408970	
	III.	Shore Ave.	Schore Ave.	
	IV.	Macon Rd.	Macon Rd.	
2.	I.	9671485	9671485	2.____
	II.	470 Astor Court	470 Astor Court	
	III.	Halprin, Phillip	Halperin, Phillip	
	IV.	Frank D. Poliseo	Frank D. Poliseo	
3.	I.	Tandem Associates	Tandom Associates	3.____
	II.	144-17 Northern Blvd.	144-17 Northern Blvd.	
	III.	Alberta Forchi	Albert Forchi	
	IV.	Kings Park, NY 10751	Kings Point, NY 10751	
4.	I.	Bertha C. McCormack	Bertha C. McCormack	4.____
	II.	Clayton, MO	Clayton, MO	
	III.	976-4242	976-4242	
	IV.	New City, NY 10951	New City, NY 10951	
5.	I.	George C. Morill	George C. Morrill	5.____
	II.	Columbia, SC 29201	Columbia, SD 29201	
	III.	Louis Ingham	Louis Ingham	
	IV.	3406 Forest Ave.	3406 Forest Ave.	
6.	I.	506 S. Elliott Pl.	506 S. Elliott Pl.	6.____
	II.	Herbert Hall	Hurbert Hall	
	III.	4712 Rockaway Pkway	4712 Rockaway Pkway	
	IV.	169 E. 7 St.	169 E. 7 St.	

7.	I.	345 Park Ave.	345 Park Pl.	7.____
	II.	Colman Oven Corp.	Coleman Oven Corp.	
	III.	Robert Conte	Robert Conti	
	IV.	6179846	6179846	
8.	I.	Grigori Schierber	Grigori Schierber	8.____
	II.	Des Moines, Iowa	Des Moines, Iowa	
	III.	Gouverneur Hospital	Gouverneur Hospital	
	IV.	91-35 Cresskill Pl.	91-35 Cresskill Pl.	
9.	I.	Jeffery Janssen	Jeffrey Janssen	9.____
	II.	8041071	8041071	
	III.	40 Rockefeller Plaza	40 Rockafeller Plaza	
	IV.	407 6 St.	406 7 St.	
10.	I.	5971996	5871996	10.____
	II.	3113 Knickerbocker Ave.	31123 Knickerbocker Ave.	
	III.	8434 Boston Post Rd.	8424 Boston Post Rd.	
	IV.	Penn Station	Penn Station	

Questions 11-14.

DIRECTIONS: Questions 11 through 14 are to be answered by looking at the four groups of names and addresses listed below (I, II, III, and IV), and then finding out the number of groups that have their corresponding numbered lies exactly the same.

	GROUP I	GROUP II
Line 1.	Richmond General Hospital	Richman General Hospital
Line 2.	Geriatric Clinic	Geriatric Clinic
Line 3.	3975 Paerdegat St.	3975 Peardegat St.
Line 4.	Loudonville, New York 11538	Londonville, New York 11538

	GROUP III	GROUP IV
Line 1.	Richmond General Hospital	Richmend General Hospital
Line 2.	Geriatric Clinic	Geriatric Clinic
Line 3.	3795 Paerdegat St.	3975 Paerdegat St.
Line 4.	Loudonville, New York 11358	Loudonville, New York 11538

1. In how many groups is line one exactly the same? 11.____
   A. Two B. Three C. Four D. None

12. In how many groups is line two exactly the same? 12.____
   A. Two B. Three C. Four D. None

13. In how many groups is line three exactly the same? 13.____
   A. Two B. Three C. Four D. None

14. In how many groups is line four exactly the same? 14.____
A. Two B. Three C. Four D. None

Questions 15-18.

DIRECTIONS: Each of Questions 15 through 18 has two lists of names and addresses. Each list contains three sets of names and addresses. Check each of the three sets in the list on the right to see if they are the same as the corresponding set in the list on the left. Mark your answers:
A. if none of the sets in the right list are the same as those in the left list
B. if only one of the sets in the right list is the same as those in the left list
C. if only two of the sets in the right list are the same as those in the left list
D. if all three sets in the right list are the same as those in the left list

15.____

15.	Mary T. Berlinger 2351 Hampton St. Monsey, N.Y. 20117	Mary T. Berlinger 2351 Hampton St. Monsey, N.Y. 20117
	Eduardo Benes 483 Kingston Avenue Central Islip, N.Y. 11734	Eduardo Benes 473 Kingston Avenue Central Islip, N.Y. 11734
	Alan Carrington Fuchs 17 Gnarled Hollow Road Los Angeles, CA 91635	Alan Carrington Fuchs 17 Gnarled Hollow Road Los Angeles, CA 91685

16.____

16.	David John Jacobson 178 34 St. Apt. 4C New York, N.Y. 00927	David John Jacobson 178 53 St. Apt. 4C New York, N.Y. 00927
	Ann-Marie Calonella 7243 South Ridge Blvd. Bakersfield, CA 96714	Ann-Marie Calonella 7243 South Ridge Blvd. Bakersfield, CA 96714
	Pauline M. Thompson 872 Linden Ave. Houston, Texas 70321	Pauline M. Thomson 872 Linden Ave. Houston, Texas 70321

17.____

17.	Chester LeRoy Masterton 152 Lacy Rd. Kankakee, Ill. 54532	Chester LeRoy Masterson 152 Lacy Rd. Kankakee, Ill. 54532
	William Maloney S. LaCrosse Pla. Wausau, Wisconsin 52136	William Maloney S. LaCross Pla. Wausau, Wisconsin 52146
	Cynthia V. Barnes 16 Pines Rd. Greenpoint, Miss. 20376	Cynthia V. Barnes 16 Pines Rd. Greenpoint,, Miss. 20376

18.	Marcel Jean Frontenac 8 Burton On The Water Calender, Me. 01471	Marcel Jean Frontenac 6 Burton On The Water Calender, Me. 01471	18.____
	J. Scott Marsden 174 S. Tipton St. Cleveland, Ohio	J. Scott Marsden 174 Tipton St. Cleveland, Ohio	
	Lawrence T. Haney 171 McDonough St. Decatur, Ga. 31304	Lawrence T. Haney 171 McDonough St. Decatur, Ga. 31304	

Questions 19-26.

DIRECTIONS: Each of Questions 19 through 26 has two lists of numbers. Each list contains three sets of numbers. Check each of the three sets in the list on the right to see if they are the same as the corresponding set in the list on the left. Mark your answers:

A. if none of the sets in the right list are the same as those in the left list
B. if only one of the sets in the right list is the same as those in the left list
C. if only two of the sets in the right list are the same as those in the left list
D. if all three sets in the right list are the same as those in the left lists

19.	7354183476 4474747744 5791430231	7354983476 4474747774 57914302311	19.____
20.	7143592185 8344517699 9178531263	7143892185 8344518699 9178531263	20.____
21.	2572114731 8806835476 8255831246	257214731 8806835476 8255831246	21.____
22.	331476853821 6976658532996 3766042113715	331476858621 6976655832996 3766042113745	22.____
23.	8806663315 74477138449 211756663666	88066633115 74477138449 211756663666	23.____

24. 990006966996 53022219743 4171171117717	99000696996 53022219843 4171171177717	24.____
25. 24400222433004 5300030055000355 20000075532002022	24400222433004 5300030055500355 20000075532002022	25.____
26. 611166640660001116 7111300117001100733 26666446664476518	61116664066001116 7111300117001100733 26666446664476518	26.____

Questions 27-30.

DIRECTIONS: Questions 27 through 30 are to be answered by picking the answer which is in the correct numerical order, from the lowest number to the highest number, in each question.

27. 27.____
A. 44533, 44518, 44516, 44547
B. 44516, 44518, 44533, 44547
C. 44547, 44533, 44518, 44516
D. 44518, 44516, 44547, 44533

28. 28.____
A. 95587, 95593, 95601, 95620
B. 95601, 95620, 95587, 95593
C. 95593, 95587, 95601. 95620
D. 95620, 95601, 95593, 95587

29. 29.____
A. 232212, 232208, 232232, 232223
B. 232208, 232223, 232212, 232232
C. 232208, 232212, 232223, 232232
D. 232223, 232232, 232208, 232208

30. 30.____
A. 113419, 113521, 113462, 113462
B. 113588, 113462, 113521, 113419
C. 113521, 113588, 113419, 113462
D. 113419, 113462, 113521, 113588

KEY (CORRECT ANSWERS)

1.	C	11.	A	21.	C
2.	B	12.	C	22.	A
3.	D	13.	A	23.	D
4.	A	14.	A	24.	A
5.	C	15.	C	25.	C
6.	B	16.	B	26.	C
7.	D	17.	B	27.	B
8.	A	18.	B	28.	A
9.	D	19.	B	29.	C
10.	C	20.	B	30.	D

RECORD KEEPING
EXAMINATION SECTION
TEST 1

DIRECTIONS: Each question or incomplete statement is followed by several suggested answers or completions. Select the one that BEST answers the question or completes the statement. *PRINT THE LETTER OF THE CORRECT ANSWER IN THE SPACE AT THE RIGHT.*

Questions 1-7.

DIRECTIONS: In answering Questions 1 through 7, use the following master list. For each question, determine where the name would fit on the master list. Each answer choice indicates right before or after the name in the answer choice.

Aaron, Jane
Armstead, Brendan
Bailey, Charles
Dent, Ricardo
Grant, Mark
Mars, Justin
Methieu, Justine
Parker, Cathy
Sampson, Suzy
Thomas, Heather

1. Schmidt, William — 1.____
   A. Right before Cathy Parker
   B. Right after Heather Thomas
   C. Right after Suzy Sampson
   D. Right before Ricardo Dent

2. Asanti, Kendall — 2.____
   A. Right before Jane Aaron
   B. Right after Charles Bailey
   C. Right before Justine Methieu
   D. Right after Brendan Armstead

3. O'Brien, Daniel — 3.____
   A. Right after Justine Methieu
   B. Right before Jane Aaron
   C. Right after Mark Grant
   D. Right before Suzy Sampson

4. Marrow, Alison — 4.____
   A. Right before Cathy Parker
   B. Right before Justin Mars
   C. Right before Mark Grant
   D. Right after Heather Thomas

5. Grantt, Marissa — 5.____
   A. Right before Mark Grant
   B. Right after Mark Grant
   C. Right after Justin Mars
   D. Right before Suzy Sampson

6. Thompson, Heath 6.____
   A. Right after Justin Mars
   B. Right before Suzy Sampson
   C. Right after Heather Thomas
   D. Right before Cathy Parker

DIRECTIONS: Before answering Question 7, add in all of the names from Questions 1 through 6. Then fit the name in alphabetical order based on the new list.

7. Francisco, Mildred 7.____
   A. Right before Mark Grant
   B. Right after Marissa Grantt
   C. Right before Alison Marrow
   D. Right after Kendall Asanti

Questions 8-10.

DIRECTIONS: In answering Questions 8 through 10, compare each pair of names and addresses. Indicate whether they are the same or different in any way.

8. William H. Pratt, J.D. / Attourney at Law — William H. Pratt, J.D. / Attorney at Law 8.____
   A. No differences
   B. 1 difference
   C. 2 differences
   D. 3 differences

9. 1303 Theater Drive,; Apt. 3-B — 1330 Theatre Drive,; Apt. 3-B 9.____
   A. No differences
   B. 1 difference
   C. 2 differences
   D. 3 differences

10. Petersdorff, Briana and Mary — Petersdorff, Briana and Mary 10.____
   A. No differences
   B. 1 difference
   C. 2 differences
   D. 3 differences

11. Which of the following words, if any, are misspelled? 11.____
   A. Affordable
   B. Circumstansial
   C. Legalese
   D. None of the above

Questions 12-13.

DIRECTIONS: Questions 12 and 13 are to be answered on the basis of the following table.

Standardized Test Results for High School Students in District #1230

	English	Math	Science	Reading
High School 1	21	22	15	18
High School 2	12	16	13	15
High School 3	16	18	21	17
High School 4	19	14	15	16

The scores for each high school in the district were averaged out and listed for each subject tested. Scores of 0-10 are significantly below College Readiness Standards. 11-15 are below College Readiness, 16-20 meet College Readiness, and 21-25 are above College Readiness.

12. If the high schools need to meet or exceed in at least half the categories in order to NOT be considered "at risk," which schools are considered "at risk"? 12.____
    A. High School 2
    B. High School 3
    C. High School 4
    D. Both A and C

13. What percentage of subjects did the district as a whole meet or exceed College Readiness standards? 13.____
    A. 25%
    B. 50%
    C. 75%
    D. 100%

Questions 14-15.

DIRECTIONS: Questions 14 and 15 are to be answered on the basis of the following information.

You have seven employees working as a part of your team: Austin, Emily, Jeremy, Christina, Martin, Harriet, and Steve. You have just sent an e-mail informing them that there will be a mandatory training session next week. To ensure that work still gets done, you are offering the training twice during the week: once on Tuesday and also on Thursday. This way half the employees will still be working while the other half attend the training. The only other issue is that Jeremy doesn't work on Tuesdays and Harriet doesn't work on Thursdays due to compressed work schedules.

14. Which of the following is a possible attendance roster for the first training session? 14.____
    A. Emily, Jeremy, Steve
    B. Steve, Christina, Harriet
    C. Harriet, Jeremy, Austin
    D. Steve, Martin, Jeremy

15. If Harriet, Christina, and Steve attend the training session on Tuesday, which of the following is a possible roster for Thursday's training session? 15.____
    A. Jeremy, Emily, and Austin
    B. Emily, Martin, and Harriet
    C. Austin, Christina, and Emily
    D. Jeremy, Emily, and Steve

Questions 16-20.

DIRECTIONS: In answering Questions 16 through 20, you will be given a word and will need to choose the answer choice that is MOST similar or different to the word.

16. Which word means the SAME as *annual*? 16.____
    A. Monthly
    B. Usually
    C. Yearly
    D. Constantly

17. Which word means the SAME as *effort*? 17.____
    A. Energy
    B. Equate
    C. Cherish
    D. Commence

18. Which word means the OPPOSITE of *forlorn*? 18.____
    A. Neglected
    B. Lethargy
    C. Optimistic
    D. Astonished

19. Which word means the SAME as *risk*? 19.____
    A. Admire
    B. Hazard
    C. Limit
    D. Hesitant

20. Which word means the OPPOSITE of *translucent*? 20.____
A. Opaque B. Transparent C. Luminous D. Introverted

21. Last year, Jamie's annual salary was $50,000. Her boss called her today to inform her that she would receive a 20% raise for the upcoming year. How much more money will Jamie receive next year? 21.____
A. $60,000 B. $10,000 C. $1,000 D. $51,000

22. You and a co-worker work for a temp hiring agency as part of their office staff. You both are given 6 days off per month. How many days off are you and your co-worker given in a year? 22.____
A. 24 B. 72 C. 144 D. 48

23. If Margot makes $34,000 per year and she works 40 hours per week for all 52 weeks, what is her hourly rate? 23.____
A. $16.34/hour B. $17.00/hour C. $15.54/hour D. $13.23/hour

24. How many dimes are there in $175.00? 24.____
A. 175 B. 1,750 C. 3,500 D. 17,500

25. If Janey is three times as old as Emily, and Emily is 3, how old is Janey? 25.____
A. 6 B. 9 C. 12 D. 15

KEY (CORRECT ANSWERS)

1.	C	11.	B
2.	D	12.	A
3.	A	13.	D
4.	B	14.	B
5.	B	15.	A
6.	C	16.	C
7.	A	17.	A
8.	B	18.	C
9.	C	19.	B
10.	A	20.	A

21.	B
22.	C
23.	A
24.	B
25.	B

TEST 2

DIRECTIONS: Each question or incomplete statement is followed by several suggested answers or completions. Select the one that BEST answers the question or completes the statement. *PRINT THE LETTER OF THE CORRECT ANSWER IN THE SPACE AT THE RIGHT.*

Questions 1-6.

DIRECTIONS: Questions 1 through 6 are to be answered on the basis of the following information.

item	name of item to be ordered
quantity	minimum number that can be ordered
beginning amount	amount in stock at start of month
amount received	amount receiving during month
ending amount	amount in stock at end of month
amount used	amount used during month
amount to order	will need at least as much of each item as used in the previous month
unit price	cost of each unit of an item
total price	total price for the order

Item	Quantity	Beginning	Received	Ending	Amount Used	Amount to Order	Unit Price	Total Price
Pens	10	22	10	8	24	20	$0.11	$2.20
Spiral notebooks	8	30	13	12			$0.25	
Binder clips	2 boxes	3 boxes	1 box	1 box			$1.79	
Sticky notes	3 packs	12 packs	4 packs	2 packs			$1.29	
Dry erase markers	1 pack (dozen)	34 markers	8 markers	40 markers			$16.49	
Ink cartridges (printer)	1 cartridge	3 cartridges	1 cartridge	2 cartridges			$79.99	
Folders	10 folders	25 folders	15 folders	10 folders			$1.08	

1. How many packs of sticky notes were used during the month? 1.____
   A. 16 B. 10 C. 12 D. 14

2. How many folders need to be ordered for next month? 2.____
   A. 15 B. 20 C. 30 D. 40

3. What is the total price of notebooks that you will need to order? 3.____
   A. $6.00 B. $0.25 C. $4.50 D. $2.75

4. Which of the following will you spend the second most money on? 4.____
   A. Ink cartridges
   B. Dry erase markers
   C. Sticky notes
   D. Binder clips

5. How many packs of dry erase markers should you order? 5.____
   A. 1 B. 8 C. 12 D. 0

6. What will be the total price of the file folders you order? 6.____
A. $20.16 B. $21.60 C. $10.80 D. $4.32

Questions 7-11.

DIRECTIONS: Questions 7 through 11 are to be answered on the basis of the following table.

Number of Car Accidents, By Location and Cause, for 2014						
	Location 1		Location 2		Location 3	
Cause	Number	Percent	Number	Percent	Number	Percent
Severe Weather	10		25		30	
Excessive Speeding	20	40	5		10	
Impaired Driving	15		15	25	8	
Miscellaneous	5		15		2	4
TOTALS	50	100	60	100	50	100

7. Which of the following is the third highest cause of accidents for all three locations? 7.____
A. Severe Weather
B. Impaired Driving
C. Miscellaneous
D. Excessive Speeding

8. The average number of Severe Weather accidents per week at Location 3 for the year (52 weeks) was MOST NEARLY 8.____
A. 0.57 B. 30 C. 1 D. 1.25

9. Which location had the LARGEST percentage of accidents caused by Impaired Driving? 9.____
A. 1 B. 2 C. 3 D. Both A and B

10. If one-third of the accidents at all three locations resulted in at least one fatality, what is the LEAST amount of deaths caused by accidents last year? 10.____
A. 60 B. 106 C. 66 D. 53

11. What is the percentage of accidents caused by miscellaneous means from all three locations in 2014? 11.____
A. 5% B. 10% C. 13% D. 25%

12. How many pairs of the following groups of letters are exactly alike? 12.____

ACDOBJ	ACDBOJ
HEWBWR	HEWRWB
DEERVS	DEERVS
BRFQSX	BRFQSX
WEYRVB	WEYRVB
SPQRZA	SQRPZA

A. 2 B. 3 C. 4 D. 5

Questions 13-19.

DIRECTIONS: Questions 13 through 19 are to be answered on the basis of the following information.

In 2012, the most current information on the American population was finished. The information was compiled by 200 volunteers in each of the 50 states. The territory of Puerto Rico, a sovereign of the United States, had 25 people assigned to compile data. In February of 2010, volunteers in each state and sovereign began collecting information. In Puerto Rico, data collection finished by January 31st, 2011, while work in the United States was completed on June 30, 2012. Each volunteer gathered data on the population of their state or sovereign. When the information was compiled, volunteers sent reports to the nation's capital, Washington, D.C. Each volunteer worked 20 hours per month and put together 10 reports per month. After the data was compiled in total, 50 people reviewed the data and worked from January 2012 to December 2012.

13. How many reports were generated from February 2010 to April 2010 in Illinois and Ohio? 13.____
A. 3,000 B. 6,000 C. 12,000 D. 15,000

14. How many volunteers in total collected population data in January 2012? 14.____
A. 10,000 B. 2,000 C. 225 D. 200

15. How many reports were put together in May 2012? 15.____
A. 2,000 B. 50,000 C. 100,000 D. 100,250

16. How many hours did the Puerto Rican volunteers work in the fall (September-November)? 16.____
A. 60 B. 500 C. 1,500 D. 0

17. How many workers were compiling or reviewing data in July 2012? 17.____
A. 25 B. 50 C. 200 D. 250

18. What was the total amount of hours worked by Nevada volunteers in July 2010? 18.____
A. 500 B. 4,000 C. 4,500 D. 5,000

19. How many reviewers worked in January 2013? 19.____
A. 75 B. 50 C. 0 D. 25

20. John has to file 10 documents per shelf. How many documents would it take for John to fill 40 shelves? 20.____
A. 40 B. 400 C. 4,500 D. 5,000

21. Jill wants to travel from New York City to Los Angeles by bike, which is approximately 2,772 miles. How many miles per day would Jill need to average if she wanted to complete the trip in 4 weeks? 21.____
A. 100 B. 89 C. 99 D. 94

22. If there are 24 CPU's and only 7 monitors, how many more monitors do you need to have the same amount of monitors as CPU's? 22.____
    A. Not enough information
    B. 17
    C. 31
    D. 0

23. If Gerry works 5 days a week and 8 hours each day, and John works 3 days a week and 10 hours each day, how many more hours per year will Gerry work than John? 23.____
    A. They work the same amount of hours.
    B. 450
    C. 520
    D. 832

24. Jimmy gets transferred to a new office. The new office has 25 employees, but only 16 are there due to a blizzard. How many coworkers was Jimmy able to meet on his first day? 24.____
    A. 16
    B. 25
    C. 9
    D. 7

25. If you do a fundraiser for charities in your area and raise $500 total, how much would you give to each charity if you were donating equal amounts to 3 of them? 25.____
    A. $250.00
    B. $167.77
    C. $50.00
    D. $111.11

KEY (CORRECT ANSWERS)

1.	D	11.	C
2.	B	12.	B
3.	A	13.	C
4.	C	14.	A
5.	D	15.	C
6.	B	16.	C
7.	D	17.	B
8.	A	18.	B
9.	A	19.	C
10.	D	20.	B

21.	C
22.	B
23.	C
24.	A
25.	B

TEST 3

DIRECTIONS: Each question or incomplete statement is followed by several suggested answers or completions. Select the one that BEST answers the question or completes the statement. *PRINT THE LETTER OF THE CORRECT ANSWER IN THE SPACE AT THE RIGHT.*

Questions 1-3.

DIRECTIONS: In answering Questions 1 through 3, choose the correctly spelled word.

1. A. allusion B. alusion C. allusien D. allution 1.____

2. A. altitude B. alltitude C. atlitude D. altlitude 2.____

3. A. althogh B. allthough C. althrough D. although 3.____

Questions 4-9.

DIRECTIONS: In answering Questions 4 through 9, choose the answer that BEST completes the analogy.

4. Odometer is to mileage as compass is to 4.____
   A. speed B. needle C. hiking D. direction

5. Marathon is to race as hibernation is to 5.____
   A. winter B. dream C. sleep D. bear

6. Cup is to coffee as bowl is to 6.____
   A. dish B. spoon C. food D. soup

7. Flow is to river as stagnant is to 7.____
   A. pool B. rain C. stream D. canal

8. Paw is to cat as hoof is to 8.____
   A. lamb B. horse C. lion D. elephant

9. Architect is to building as sculptor is to 9.____
   A. museum B. chisel C. stone D. statue

Questions 10-14.

DIRECTIONS: Questions 10 through 14 are to be answered on the basis of the following graph.

Population of Carroll City Broken Down by Age and Gender (in Thousands)			
Age	Female	Male	Total
Under 15	60	60	120
15-23		22	
24-33		20	44
34-43	13	18	31
44-53	20		67
64 and Over	65	65	130
TOTAL	230	232	462

10. How many people in the city are between the ages of 15-23? 10.____
    A. 70 B. 46,000 C. 70,000 D. 225,000

11. Approximately what percentage of the total population of the city was female aged 24-33? 11.____
    A. 10% B. 5% C. 15% D. 25%

12. If 33% of the males have a job and 55% of females don't have a job, which of the following statements is TRUE? 12.____
    A. Males have approximately 2,600 more jobs than females.
    B. Females have approximately 49,000 more jobs than males.
    C. Females have approximately 26,000 more jobs than males.
    D. None of the above statements are true.

13. How many females between the ages of 15-23 live in Carroll City? 13.____
    A. 67,000 B. 24,000 C. 48,000 D. 91,000

14. Assume all males 44-53 living in Carroll City are employed. If two-thirds of males age 44-53 work jobs outside of Carroll City, how many work within city limits? 14.____
    A. 31,333
    B. 15,667
    C. 47,000
    D. Cannot answer the question with the information provided

Questions 15-16.

DIRECTIONS: Questions 15 and 16 are labeled as shown. Alphabetize them for filing. Choose the answer that correctly shows the order.

15. (1) AED
(2) OOS
(3) FOA
(4) DOM
(5) COB

A. 2-5-4-3-2 B. 1-4-5-2-3 C. 1-5-4-2-3 D. 1-5-4-3-2

15.____

16. Alphabetize the names of the people. Last names are given last.
(1) Lindsey Jamestown
(2) Jane Alberta
(3) Ally Jamestown
(4) Allison Johnston
(5) Lyle Moreno

A. 2-1-3-4-5 B. 3-4-2-1-5 C. 2-3-1-4-5 D. 4-3-2-1-5

16.____

17. Which of the following words is misspelled?
A. disgust
B. whisper
C. locale
D. none of the above

17.____

Questions 18-21.

DIRECTIONS: Questions 18 through 21 are to be answered on the basis of the following list of employees.

Robertson, Aaron
Bacon, Gina
Jerimiah, Trace
Gillette, Stanley
Jacks, Sharon

18. Which employee name would come in third in alphabetized list?
A. Robertson, Aaron
B. Jerimiah, Trace
C. Gillette, Stanley
D. Jacks, Sharon

18.____

19. Which employee's first name starts with the letter in the alphabet that is five letters after the first letter of their last name?
A. Jerimiah, Trace
B. Bacon, Gina
C. Jacks, Sharon
D. Gillette, Stanley

19.____

20. How many employees have last names that are exactly five letters long?
A. 1 B. 2 C. 3 D. 4

20.____

21. How many of the employees have either a first or last name that starts with the letter "G"? 21.____
A. 1 B. 2 C. 4 D. 5

Questions 22-25.

DIRECTIONS: Questions 22 through 25 are to be answered on the basis of the following chart.

Bicycle Sales (Model #34JA32)							
Country	May	June	July	August	September	October	Total
Germany	34	47	45	54	56	60	296
Britain	40	44	36	47	47	46	260
Ireland	37	32	32	32	34	33	200
Portugal	14	14	14	16	17	14	89
Italy	29	29	28	31	29	31	177
Belgium	22	24	24	26	25	23	144
Total	176	198	179	206	208	207	1166

22. What percentage of the overall total was sold to the German importer? 22.____
A. 25.3% B. 22% C. 24.1% D. 23%

23. What percentage of the overall total was sold in September? 23.____
A. 24.1% B. 25.6% C. 17.9% D. 24.6%

24. What is the average number of units per month imported into Belgium over the first four months shown? 24.____
A. 26 B. 20 C. 24 D. 31

25. If you look at the three smallest importers, what is their total import percentage? 25.____
A. 35.1% B. 37.1% C. 40% D. 28%

KEY (CORRECT ANSWERS)

1. A
2. A
3. D
4. D
5. C

6. D
7. A
8. B
9. D
10. C

11. B
12. C
13. C
14. B
15. D

16. C
17. D
18. D
19. B
20. B

21. B
22. A
23. C
24. C
25. A

TEST 4

DIRECTIONS: Each question or incomplete statement is followed by several suggested answers or completions. Select the one that BEST answers the question or completes the statement. *PRINT THE LETTER OF THE CORRECT ANSWER IN THE SPACE AT THE RIGHT.*

Questions 1-6.

DIRECTIONS: In answering Questions 1 through 6, choose the sentence that represents the BEST example of English grammar.

1. A. Joey and me want to go on a vacation next week. 1.____
   B. Gary told Jim he would need to take some time off.
   C. If turning six years old, Jim's uncle would teach Spanish to him.
   D. Fax a copy of your resume to Ms. Perez and me.

2. A. Jerry stood in line for almost two hours. 2.____
   B. The reaction to my engagement was less exciting than I thought it would be.
   C. Carlos and me have done great work on this project.
   D. Two parts of the speech needs to be revised before tomorrow.

3. A. Arriving home, the alarm was tripped. 3.____
   B. Jonny is regarded as a stand up guy, a responsible parent, and he doesn't give up until a task is finished.
   C. Each employee must submit a drug test each month.
   D. One of the documents was incinerated in the explosion.

4. A. As soon as my parents get home, I told them I finished all of my chores. 4.____
   B. I asked my teacher to send me my missing work, check my absences, and how did I do on my test.
   C. Matt attempted to keep it concealed from Jenny and me.
   D. If Mary or him cannot get work done on time, I will have to split them up.

5. A. Driving to work, the traffic report warned him of an accident on Highway 47. 5.____
   B. Jimmy has performed well this season.
   C. Since finishing her degree, several job offers have been given to Cam.
   D. Our boss is creating unstable conditions for we employees.

6. A. The thief was described as a tall man with a wiry mustache weighing approximately 150 pounds. 6.____
   B. She gave Patrick and I some more time to finish our work.
   C. One of the books that he ordered was damaged in shipping.
   D. While talking on the rotary phone, the car Jim was driving skidded off the road.

Questions 7-9.

DIRECTIONS: Questions 7 through 9 are to be answered on the basis of the following graph.

Ice Lake Frozen Flight (2002-2013)		
Year	Number of Participants	Temperature (Fahrenheit)
2002	22	4°
2003	50	33°
2004	69	18°
2005	104	22°
2006	108	24°
2007	288	33°
2008	173	9°
2009	598	39°
2010	698	26°
2011	696	30°
2012	777	28°
2013	578	32°

7. Which two year span had the LARGEST difference between temperatures? 7.____
   A. 2002 and 2003
   B. 2011 and 2012
   C. 2008 and 2009
   D. 2003 and 2004

8. How many total people participated in the years after the temperature reached at least 29°? 8.____
   A. 2,295
   B. 1,717
   C. 2,210
   D. 4,543

9. In 2007, the event saw 288 participants, while in 2008 that number dropped to 173. Which of the following reasons BEST explains the drop in participants? 9.____
   A. The event had not been going on that long and people didn't know about it.
   B. The lake water wasn't cold enough to have people jump in.
   C. The temperature was too cold for many people who would have normally participated.
   D. None of the above reasons explain the drop in participants.

10. In the following list of numbers, how many times does 4 come just after 2 when 2 comes just after an odd number? 10.____
    2365247653898632488572486392424
    A. 2
    B. 3
    C. 4
    D. 5

11. Which choice below lists the letter that is as far after B as S is after N in the alphabet? 11.____
    A. G
    B. H
    C. I
    D. J

Questions 12-15.

DIRECTIONS: Questions 12 through 15 are to be answered on the basis of the following directory and list of changes.

Directory		
Name	Emp. Type	Position
Julie Taylor	Warehouse	Packer
James King	Office	Administrative Assistant
John Williams	Office	Salesperson
Ray Moore	Warehouse	Maintenance
Kathleen Byrne	Warehouse	Supervisor
Amy Jones	Office	Salesperson
Paul Jonas	Office	Salesperson
Lisa Wong	Warehouse	Loader
Eugene Lee	Office	Accountant
Bruce Lavine	Office	Manager
Adam Gates	Warehouse	Packer
Will Suter	Warehouse	Packer
Gary Lorper	Office	Accountant
Jon Adams	Office	Salesperson
Susannah Harper	Office	Salesperson

Directory Updates:

- Employee e-mail addresses will adhere to the following guidelines: lastnamefirstname@apexindustries.com (ex. Susannah Harper is harpersusannah@apexindustries.com). Currently, employees in the warehouse share one e-mail, distribution@apexindustries.com.
- The "Loader" position will now be referred to as "Specialist I"
- Adam Gates has accepted a Supervisor position within the Warehouse and is no longer a Packer. All warehouse employees report to the two Supervisors and all office employees report to the Manager.

12. Amy Jones tried to send an e-mail to Adam Gates, but it wouldn't send. Which of the following offers the BEST explanation? 12.____
    A. Amy put Adam's first name first and then his last name.
    B. Adam doesn't check his e-mail, so he wouldn't know if he received the e-mail or not.
    C. Adam does not have his own e-mail.
    D. Office employees are not allowed to send e-mails to each other.

13. How many Packers currently work for Apex Industries? 13.____
    A. 2   B. 3   C. 4   D. 5

14. What position does Lisa Wong currently hold? 14.____
    A. Specialist I   B. Secretary
    C. Administrative Assistant   D. Loader

15. If an employee wanted to contact the office manager, which of the following e-mails should the e-mail be sent to? 15.____
    A. officemanager@apexindustries.com
    B. brucelavine@apexindustries.com
    C. lavinebruce@apexindustries.com
    D. distribution@apexindustries.com

Questions 16-19.

DIRECTIONS: In answering Questions 16 through 19, compare the three names, numbers or addresses.

16. Smiley Yarnell Smiley Yarnel Smily Yarnell 16.____
    A. All three are exactly alike.
    B. The first and second are exactly alike.
    C. The second and third are exactly alike.
    D. All three are different.

17. 1583 Theater Drive 1583 Theater Drive 1583 Theatre Drive 17.____
    A. All three are exactly alike.
    B. The first and second are exactly alike.
    C. The second and third are exactly alike.
    D. All three are different.

18. 3341893212 3341893212 3341893212 18.____
    A. All three are exactly alike.
    B. The first and second are exactly alike.
    C. The second and third are exactly alike.
    D. All three are different.

19. Douglass Watkins Douglas Watkins Douglass Watkins 19.____
    A. All three are exactly alike.
    B. The first and third are exactly alike.
    C. The second and third are exactly alike.
    D. All three are different.

Questions 20-24.

DIRECTIONS: In answering Questions 20 through 24, you will be presented with a word. Choose the synonym that BEST represents the word in question.

20. Flexible 20.____
    A. delicate B. inflammable C. strong D. pliable

21. Alternative 21.____
    A. choice B. moderate C. lazy D. value

22. Corroborate — 22.____
    A. examine B. explain C. verify D. explain

23. Respiration — 23.____
    A. recovery B. breathing C. sweating D. selfish

24. Negligent — 24.____
    A. lazy B. moderate C. hopeless D. lax

25. Plumber is to Wrench as Painter is to — 25.____
    A. pipe B. shop C. hammer D. brush

KEY (CORRECT ANSWERS)

1.	D	11.	A
2.	A	12.	C
3.	D	13.	A
4.	C	14.	A
5.	B	15.	C
6.	C	16.	D
7.	C	17.	B
8.	B	18.	A
9.	C	19.	B
10.	C	20.	D

21.	A
22.	C
23.	B
24.	D
25.	D

PHILOSOPHY, PRINCIPLES, PRACTICES, AND TECHNICS OF SUPERVISION, ADMINISTRATION, MANAGEMENT, AND ORGANIZATION

TABLE OF CONTENTS

PHILOSOPHY, PRINCIPLES, PRACTICES, AND TECHNICS
OF
SUPERVISION, ADMINISTRATION, MANAGEMENT, AND ORGANIZATION

MEANING OF SUPERVISION

The extension of the democratic philosophy has been accompanied by an extension in the scope of supervision. Modern leaders and supervisors no longer think of supervision in the narrow sense of being confined chiefly to visiting employees, supplying materials, or rating the staff. They regard supervision as being intimately related to all the concerned agencies of society, they speak of the supervisor's function in terms of "growth," rather than the "improvement" of employees.

This modern concept of supervision may be defined as follows: Supervision is leadership and the development of leadership within groups which are cooperatively engaged in inspection, research, training, guidance, and evaluation.

THE OLD AND THE NEW SUPERVISION

TRADITIONAL
1. Inspection
2. Focused on the employee
3. Visitation
4. Random and haphazard
5. Imposed and authoritarian
6. One person usually

MODERN
1. Study and analysis
2. Focused on aims, materials, methods, supervisors, employees, environment
3. Demonstrations, intervisitation, workshops, directed reading, bulletins, etc.
4. Definitely organized and planned (scientific)
5. Cooperative and democratic
6. Many persons involved (creative)

THE EIGHT (8) BASIC PRINCIPLES OF THE NEW SUPERVISION

I. Principle of Responsibility
Authority to act and responsibility for acting must be joined.
   A. If you give responsibility, give authority.
   B. Define employee duties clearly.
   C. Protect employees from criticism by others.
   D. Recognize the rights as well as obligations of employees.
   E. Achieve the aims of a democratic society insofar as it is possible within the area of your work.
   F. Establish a situation favorable to training and learning.
   G. Accept ultimate responsibility for everything done in your section, unit, office, division, department.
   H. Good administration and good supervision are inseparable.

II. Principle of Authority
The success of the supervisor is measured by the extent to which the power of authority is not used.
A. Exercise simplicity and informality in supervision
B. Use the simplest machinery of supervision
C. If it is good for the organization as a whole, it is probably justified.
D. Seldom be arbitrary or authoritative.
E. Do not base your work on the power of position or of personality.
F. Permit and encourage the free expression of opinions.

III. Principle of Self-Growth
The success of the supervisor is measured by the extent to which, and the speed with which, he is no longer needed.
A. Base criticism on principles, not on specifics.
B. Point out higher activities to employees.
C. Train for self-thinking by employees to meet new situations.
D. Stimulate initiative, self-reliance, and individual responsibility
E. Concentrate on stimulating the growth of employees rather than on removing defects.

IV. Principle of Individual Worth
Respect for the individual is a paramount consideration in supervision.
A. Be human and sympathetic in dealing with employees.
B. Don't nag about things to be done.
C. Recognize the individual differences among employees and seek opportunities to permit best expression of each personality.

V. Principle of Creative Leadership
The best supervision is that which is not apparent to the employee.
A. Stimulate, don't drive employees to creative action.
B. Emphasize doing good things.
C. Encourage employees to do what they do best.
D. Do not be too greatly concerned with details of subject or method.
E. Do not be concerned exclusively with immediate problems and activities.
F. Reveal higher activities and make them both desired and maximally possible.
G. Determine procedures in the light of each situation but see that these are derived from a sound basic philosophy.
H. Aid, inspire, and lead so as to liberate the creative spirit latent in all good employees.

VI. Principle of Success and Failure
There are no unsuccessful employees, only unsuccessful supervisors who have failed to give proper leadership.
A. Adapt suggestions to the capacities, attitudes, and prejudices of employees.
B. Be gradual, be progressive, be persistent.
C. Help the employee find the general principle; have the employee apply his own problem to the general principle.
D. Give adequate appreciation for good work and honest effort.
E. Anticipate employee difficulties and help to prevent them.
F. Encourage employees to do the desirable things they will do anyway.
G. Judge your supervision by the results it secures.

VII. Principle of Science
Successful supervision is scientific, objective, and experimental. It is based on facts, not on prejudices.
A. Be cumulative in results.
B. Never divorce your suggestions from the goals of training.
C. Don't be impatient of results.
D. Keep all matters on a professional, not a personal, level.
E. Do not be concerned exclusively with immediate problems and activities.
F. Use objective means of determining achievement and rating where possible.

VIII. Principle of Cooperation
Supervision is a cooperative enterprise between supervisor and employee.
A. Begin with conditions as they are.
B. Ask opinions of all involved when formulating policies.
C. Organization is as good as its weakest link.
D. Let employees help to determine policies and department programs.
E. Be approachable and accessible—physically and mentally.
F. Develop pleasant social relationships.

WHAT IS ADMINISTRATION

Administration is concerned with providing the environment, the material facilities, and the operational procedures that will promote the maximum growth and development of supervisors and employees. (Organization is an aspect and a concomitant of administration.)

There is no sharp line of demarcation between supervision and administration; these functions are intimately interrelated and, often, overlapping. They are complementary activities.

I. Practices Commonly Classed as "Supervisory"
A. Conducting employees' conferences
B. Visiting sections, units, offices, divisions, departments
C. Arranging for demonstrations
D. Examining plans
E. Suggesting professional reading
F. Interpreting bulletins
G. Recommending in-service training courses
H. Encouraging experimentation
I. Appraising employee morale
J. Providing for intervisitation

II. Practices Commonly Classified as "Administrative"
A. Management of the office
B. Arrangement of schedules for extra duties
C. Assignment of rooms or areas
D. Distribution of supplies
E. Keeping records and reports
F. Care of audio-visual materials
G. Keeping inventory records
H. Checking record cards and books

I. Programming special activities
J. Checking on the attendance and punctuality of employees

III. Practices Commonly Classified as Both "Supervisory" and "Administrative"
A. Program construction
B. Testing or evaluating outcomes
C. Personnel accounting
D. Ordering instructional materials

RESPONSIBILITIES OF THE SUPERVISOR

A person employed in a supervisory capacity must constantly be able to improve his own efficiency and ability. He represent the employer to the employees and only continuous self-examination can make him a capable supervisor.

Leadership and training are the supervisor's responsibility. An efficient working unit is one in which the employees work with the supervisor. It is his job to bring out the best in his employees. He must always be relaxed, courteous, and calm in his association with his employees. Their feelings are important, and a harsh attitude does not develop the most efficient employees.

COMPETENCES OF THE SUPERVISOR

I. Complete knowledge of the duties and responsibilities of his position.
II. To be able to organize a job, plan ahead, and carry through.
III. To have self-confidence and initiative.
IV. To be able to handle the unexpected situation and make quick decisions.
V. To be able to properly train subordinates in the positions they are best suited for.
VI. To be able to keep good human relations among his subordinates.
VII. To be able to keep good human relations between his subordinates and himself and to earn their respect and trust.

THE PROFESSIONAL SUPERVISOR-EMPLOYEE RELATIONSHIP

There are two kinds of efficiency: one kind is only apparent and is produced in organizations through the exercise of mere discipline; this is but a simulation of the second, or true, efficiency which springs from spontaneous cooperation. If you are a manager, no matter how great or small your responsibility, it is your job, in the final analysis, to create and develop this involuntary cooperation among the people whom you supervise. For, no matter how powerful a combination of money, machines, and materials a company may have, this is a dead and sterile thing without a team of willing, thinking, and articulate people to guide it.

The following 21 points are presented as indicative of the exemplary basic relationship that should exist between supervisor and employee:

1. Each person wants to be liked and respected by his fellow employee and wants to be treated with consideration and respect by his superior.
2. The most competent employee will make an error. However, in a unit where good relations exist between the supervisor and his employees, tenseness and fear do not exist. Thus, errors are not hidden or covered up, and the efficiency of a unit is not impaired.

3. Subordinates resent rules, regulations, or orders that are unreasonable or unexplained.
4. Subordinates are quick to resent unfairness, harshness, injustices, and favoritism.
5. An employee will accept responsibility if he knows that he will be complimented for a job well done, and not too harshly chastised for failure; that his supervisor will check the cause of the failure, and, if it was the supervisor's fault, he will assume the blame therefore. If it was the employee's fault, his supervisor will explain the correct method or means of handling the responsibility.
6. An employee wants to receive credit for a suggestion he has made, that is used. If a suggestion cannot be used, the employee is entitled to an explanation. The supervisor should not say "no" and close the subject.
7. Fear and worry slow up a worker's ability. Poor working environment can impair his physical and mental health. A good supervisor avoids forceful methods, threats, and arguments to get a job done.
8. A forceful supervisor is able to train his employees individually and as a team, and is able to motivate them in the proper channels.
9. A mature supervisor is able to properly evaluate his subordinates and to keep them happy and satisfied.
10. A sensitive supervisor will never patronize his subordinates.
11. A worthy supervisor will respect his employees' confidences.
12. Definite and clear-cut responsibilities should be assigned to each executive.
13. Responsibility should always be coupled with corresponding authority.
14. No change should be made in the scope or responsibilities of a position without a definite understanding to that effect on the part of all persons concerned.
15. No executive or employee, occupying a single position in the organization, should be subject to definite orders from more than one source.
16. Orders should never be given to subordinates over the head of a responsible executive. Rather than do this, the officer in question should be supplanted.
17. Criticisms of subordinates should, whoever possible, be made privately, and in no case should a subordinate be criticized in the presence of executives or employees of equal or lower rank.
18. No dispute or difference between executives or employees as to authority or responsibilities should be considered too trivial for prompt and careful adjudication.
19. Promotions, wage changes, and disciplinary action should always be approved by the executive immediately superior to the one directly responsible.
20. No executive or employee should ever be required, or expected, to be at the same time an assistant to, and critic of, another.
21. Any executive whose work is subject to regular inspection should, wherever practicable, be given the assistance and facilities necessary to enable him to maintain an independent check of the quality of his work.

MINI-TEXT IN SUPERVISION, ADMINISTRATION, MANAGEMENT, AND ORGANIZATION

I. Brief Highlights

Listed concisely and sequentially are major headings and important data in the field for quick recall and review.

A. Levels of Management

Any organization of some size has several levels of management. In terms of a ladder, the levels are:

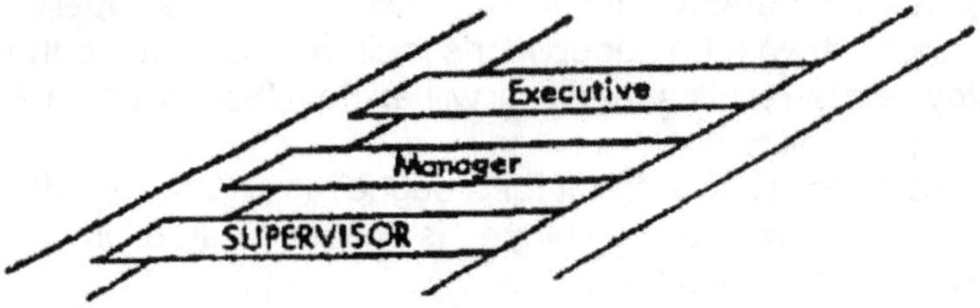

The first level is very important because it is the beginning point of management leadership.

B. What the Supervisor Must Learn

A supervisor must learn to:

1. Deal with people and their differences
2. Get the job done through people
3. Recognize the problems when they exist
4. Overcome obstacles to good performance
5. Evaluate the performance of people
6. Check his own performance in terms of accomplishment

C. A Definition of Supervisor

The term supervisor means any individual having authority, in the interests of the employer, to hire, transfer, suspend, lay-off, recall, promote, discharge, assign, reward, or discipline other employees or responsibility to direct them, or to adjust their grievances, or effectively to recommend such action, if, in connection with the foregoing, exercise of such authority is not of a merely routine or clerical nature but requires the use of independent judgment.

D. Elements of the Team Concept

What is involved in teamwork? The component parts are:

1. Members
2. A leader
3. Goals
4. Plans
5. Cooperation
6. Spirit

E. Principles of Organization

1. A team member must know what his job is.
2. Be sure that the nature and scope of a job are understood.
3. Authority and responsibility should be carefully spelled out.
4. A supervisor should be permitted to make the maximum number of decisions affecting his employees.
5. Employees should report to only one supervisor.
6. A supervisor should direct only as many employees as he can handle effectively.
7. An organization plan should be flexible.

8. Inspection and performance of work should be separate.
9. Organizational problems should receive immediate attention.
10. Assign work in line with ability and experience.

F. The Four Important Parts of Every Job

1. Inherent in every job is the *accountability* for results.
2. A second set of factors in every job is *responsibilities.*
3. Along with duties and responsibilities one must have the *authority* to act within certain limits without obtaining permission to proceed.
4. No job exists in a vacuum. The supervisor is surrounded by key *relationships.*

G. Principles of Delegation

Where work is delegated for the first time, the supervisor should think in terms of these questions:

1. Who is best qualified to do this?
2. Can an employee improve his abilities by doing this?
3. How long should an employee spend on this?
4. Are there any special problems for which he will need guidance?
5. How broad a delegation can I make?

H. Principles of Effective Communications

1. Determine the media.
2. To whom directed?
3. Identification and source authority.
4. Is communication understood?

I. Principles of Work Improvement

1. Most people usually do only the work which is assigned to them.
2. Workers are likely to fit assigned work into the time available to perform it.
3. A good workload usually stimulates output.
4. People usually do their best work when they know that results will be reviewed or inspected.
5. Employees usually feel that someone else is responsible for conditions of work, workplace layout, job methods, type of tools/equipment, and other such factors.
6. Employees are usually defensive about their job security.
7. Employees have natural resistance to change.
8. Employees can support or destroy a supervisor.
9. A supervisor usually earns the respect of his people through his personal example of diligence and efficiency.

J. Areas of Job Improvement

The areas of job improvement are quite numerous, but the most common ones which a supervisor can identify and utilize are:

1. Departmental layout
2. Flow of work
3. Workplace layout
4. Utilization of manpower
5. Work methods
6. Materials handling

7. Utilization
8. Motion economy

K. Seven Key Points in Making Improvements
1. Select the job to be improved
2. Study how it is being done now
3. Question the present method
4. Determine actions to be taken
5. Chart proposed method
6. Get approval and apply
7. Solicit worker participation

I. Corrective Techniques of Job Improvement

Specific Problems
1. Size of workload
2. Inability to meet schedules
3. Strain and fatigue
4. Improper use of men and skills
5. Waste, poor quality, unsafe conditions
6. Bottleneck conditions that hinder output
7. Poor utilization of equipment and machine
8. Efficiency and productivity of labor

General Improvement
1. Departmental layout
2. Flow of work
3. Work plan layout
4. Utilization of manpower
5. Work methods
6. Materials handling
7. Utilization of equipment
8. Motion economy

Corrective Techniques
1. Study with scale model
2. Flow chart study
3. Motion analysis
4. Comparison of units produced to standard allowance
5. Methods analysis
6. Flow chart and equipment study
7. Down time vs. running time
8. Motion analysis

M. A Planning Checklist
1. Objectives
2. Controls
3. Delegations
4. Communications
5. Resources
6. Manpower

7. Equipment
8. Supplies and materials
9. Utilization of time
10. Safety
11. Money
12. Work
13. Timing of improvements

N. Five Characteristics of Good Directions

In order to get results, directions must be:

1. Possible of accomplishment
2. Agreeable with worker interests
3. Related to mission
4. Planned and complete
5. Unmistakably clear

O. Types of Directions

1. Demands or direct orders
2. Requests
3. Suggestion or implication
4. volunteering

P. Controls

A typical listing of the overall areas in which the supervisor should establish controls might be:

1. Manpower
2. Materials
3. Quality of work
4. Quantity of work
5. Time
6. Space
7. Money
8. Methods

Q. Orienting the New Employee

1. Prepare for him
2. Welcome the new employee
3. Orientation for the job
4. Follow-up

R. Checklist for Orienting New Employees

	Yes	No
1. Do you appreciate the feelings of new employees when they first report for work?	___	___
2. Are you aware of the fact that the new employee must make a big adjustment to his job?	___	___
3. Have you given him good reasons for liking the job and the organization?	___	___
4. Have you prepared for his first day on the job?	___	___
5. Did you welcome him cordially and make him feel needed?	___	___

		Yes	No
6.	Did you establish rapport with him so that he feels free to talk and discuss matters with you?	___	___
7.	Did you explain his job to him and his relationship to you?	___	___
8.	Does he know that his work will be evaluated periodically on a basis that is fair and objective?	___	___
9.	Did you introduce him to his fellow workers in such a way that they are likely to accept him?	___	___
10.	Does he know what employee benefits he will receive?	___	___
11.	Does he understand the importance of being on the job and what to do if he must leave his duty station?	___	___
12.	Has he been impressed with the importance of accident prevention and safe practice?	___	___
13.	Does he generally know his way around the department?	___	___
14.	Is he under the guidance of a sponsor who will teach the right way of doing things?	___	___
15.	Do you plan to follow-up so that he will continue to adjust successfully to his job?	___	___

S. Principles of Learning
1. Motivation
2. Demonstration or explanation
3. Practice

T. Causes of Poor Performance
1. Improper training for job
2. Wrong tools
3. Inadequate directions
4. Lack of supervisory follow-up
5. Poor communications
6. Lack of standards of performance
7. Wrong work habits
8. Low morale
9. Other

U. Four Major Steps in On-The-Job Instruction
1. Prepare the worker
2. Present the operation
3. Tryout performance
4. Follow-up

V. Employees Want Five Things
1. Security
2. Opportunity
3. Recognition
4. Inclusion
5. Expression

W. Some Don'ts in Regard to Praise
1. Don't praise a person for something he hasn't done.
2. Don't praise a person unless you can be sincere.
3. Don't be sparing in praise just because your superior withholds it from you.
4. Don't let too much time elapse between good performance and recognition of it

X. How to Gain Your Workers' Confidence
Methods of developing confidence include such things as:
1. Knowing the interests, habits, hobbies of employees
2. Admitting your own inadequacies
3. Sharing and telling of confidence in others
4. Supporting people when they are in trouble
5. Delegating matters that can be well handled
6. Being frank and straightforward about problems and working conditions
7. Encouraging others to bring their problems to you
8. Taking action on problems which impede worker progress

Y. Sources of Employee Problems
On-the-job causes might be such things as:
1. A feeling that favoritism is exercised in assignments
2. Assignment of overtime
3. An undue amount of supervision
4. Changing methods or systems
5. Stealing of ideas or trade secrets
6. Lack of interest in job
7. Threat of reduction in force
8. Ignorance or lack of communications
9. Poor equipment
10. Lack of knowing how supervisor feels toward employee
11. Shift assignments

Off-the-job problems might have to do with:
1. Health
2. Finances
3. Housing
4. Family

Z. The Supervisor's Key to Discipline
There are several key points about discipline which the supervisor should keep in mind:
1. Job discipline is one of the disciplines of life and is directed by the supervisor.
2. It is more important to correct an employee fault than to fix blame for it.
3. Employee performance is affected by problems both on the job and off.
4. Sudden or abrupt changes in behavior can be indications of important employee problems.
5. Problems should be dealt with as soon as possible after they are identified.
6. The attitude of the supervisor may have more to do with solving problems than the techniques of problem solving.
7. Correction of employee behavior should be resorted to only after the supervisor is sure that training or counseling will not be helpful.

8. Be sure to document your disciplinary actions.
9. Make sure that you are disciplining on the basis of facts rather than personal feelings.
10. Take each disciplinary step in order, being careful not to make snap judgments, or decisions based on impatience.

AA. Five Important Processes of Management
1. Planning
2. Organizing
3. Scheduling
4. Controlling
5. Motivating

BB. When the Supervisor Fails to Plan
1. Supervisor creates impression of not knowing his job
2. May lead to excessive overtime
3. Job runs itself—supervisor lacks control
4. Deadlines and appointments missed
5. Parts of the work go undone
6. Work interrupted by emergencies
7. Sets a bad example
8. Uneven workload creates peaks and valleys
9. Too much time on minor details at expense of more important tasks

CC. Fourteen General Principles of Management
1. Division of work
2. Authority and responsibility
3. Discipline
4. Unity of command
5. Unity of direction
6. Subordination of individual interest to general interest
7. Remuneration of personnel
8. Centralization
9. Scalar chain
10. Order
11. Equity
12. Stability of tenure of personnel
13. Initiative
14. Esprit de corps

DD. Change

Bringing about change is perhaps attempted more often, and yet less well understood, than anything else the supervisor does. How do people generally react to change? (People tend to resist change that is imposed upon them by other individuals or circumstances.

Change is characteristic of every situation. It is a part of every real endeavor where the efforts of people are concerned.

1. Why do people resist change?
   People may resist change because of:
   a. Fear of the unknown
   b. Implied criticism
   c. Unpleasant experiences in the past
   d. Fear of loss of status
   e. Threat to the ego
   f. Fear of loss of economic stability

2. How can we best overcome the resistance to change?
   In initiating change, take these steps:
   a. Get ready to sell
   b. Identify sources of help
   c. Anticipate objections
   d. Sell benefits
   e. Listen in depth
   f. Follow up

II. Brief Topical Summaries

A. Who/What is the Supervisor?
   1. The supervisor is often called the "highest level employee and the lowest level manager."
   2. A supervisor is a member of both management and the work group. He acts as a bridge between the two.
   3. Most problems in supervision are in the area of human relations, or people problems.
   4. Employees expect: Respect, opportunity to learn and to advance, and a sense of belonging, and so forth.
   5. Supervisors are responsible for directing people and organizing work. Planning is of paramount importance.
   6. A position description is a set of duties and responsibilities inherent to a given position.
   7. It is important to keep the position description up-to-date and to provide each employee with his own copy.

B. The Sociology of Work
   1. People are alike in many ways; however, each individual is unique.
   2. The supervisor is challenged in getting to know employee differences. Acquiring skills in evaluating individuals is an asset.
   3. Maintaining meaningful working relationships in the organization is of great importance.
   4. The supervisor has an obligation to help individuals to develop to their fullest potential.
   5. Job rotation on a planned basis helps to build versatility and to maintain interest and enthusiasm in work groups.
   6. Cross training (job rotation) provides backup skills.

7. The supervisor can help reduce tension by maintaining a sense of humor, providing guidance to employees, and by making reasonable and timely decisions. Employees respond favorably to working under reasonably predictable circumstances.
8. Change is characteristic of all managerial behavior. The supervisor must adjust to changes in procedures, new methods, technological changes, and to a number of new and sometimes challenging situations.
9. To overcome the natural tendency for people to resist change, the supervisor should become more skillful in initiating change.

C. Principles and Practices of Supervision

1. Employees should be required to answer to only one superior.
2. A supervisor can effectively direct only a limited number of employees, depending upon the complexity, variety, and proximity of the jobs involved.
3. The organizational chart presents the organization in graphic form. It reflects lines of authority and responsibility as well as interrelationships of units within the organization.
4. Distribution of work can be improved through an analysis using the "Work Distribution Chart."
5. The "Work Distribution Chart" reflects the division of work within a unit in understandable form.
6. When related tasks are given to an employee, he has a better chance of increasing his skills through training.
7. The individual who is given the responsibility for tasks must also be given the appropriate authority to insure adequate results.
8. The supervisor should delegate repetitive, routine work. Preparation of recurring reports, maintaining leave and attendance records are some examples.
9. Good discipline is essential to good task performance. Discipline is reflected in the actions of employees on the job in the absence of supervision.
10. Disciplinary action may have to be taken when the positive aspects of discipline have failed. Reprimand, warning, and suspension are examples of disciplinary action.
11. If a situation calls for a reprimand, be sure it is deserved and remember it is to be done in private.

D. Dynamic Leadership

1. A style is a personal method or manner of exerting influence.
2. Authoritarian leaders often see themselves as the source of power and authority.
3. The democratic leader often perceives the group as the source of authority and power.
4. Supervisors tend to do better when using the pattern of leadership that is most natural for them.
5. Social scientists suggest that the effective supervisor use the leadership style that best fits the problem or circumstances involved.
6. All four styles—telling, selling, consulting, joining—have their place. Using one does not preclude using the other at another time.

7. The theory X point of view assumes that the average person dislikes work, will avoid it whenever possible, and must be coerced to achieve organizational objectives.
8. The theory Y point of view assumes that the average person considers work to be a natural as play, and, when the individual is committed, he requires little supervision or direction to accomplish desired objectives.
9. The leader's basic assumptions concerning human behavior and human nature affect his actions, decisions, and other managerial practices.
10. Dissatisfaction among employees is often present, but difficult to isolate. The supervisor should seek to weaken dissatisfaction by keeping promises, being sincere and considerate, keeping employees informed, and so forth.
11. Constructive suggestions should be encouraged during the natural progress of the work.

E. Processes for Solving Problems

1. People find their daily tasks more meaningful and satisfying when they can improve them.
2. The causes of problems, or the key factors, are often hidden in the background. Ability to solve problems often involves the ability to isolate them from their backgrounds. There is some substance to the cliché that some persons "can't see the forest for the trees."
3. New procedures are often developed from old ones. Problems should be broken down into manageable parts. New ideas can be adapted from old one.
4. People think differently in problem-solving situations. Using a logical, patterned approach is often useful. One approach found to be useful includes these steps:
   a. Define the problem
   b. Establish objectives
   c. Get the facts
   d. Weigh and decide
   e. Take action
   f. Evaluate action

F. Training for Results

1. Participants respond best when they feel training is important to them.
2. The supervisor has responsibility for the training and development of those who report to him.
3. When training is delegated to others, great care must be exercised to insure the trainer has knowledge, aptitude, and interest for his work as a trainer.
4. Training (learning) of some type goes on continually. The most successful supervisor makes certain the learning contributes in a productive manner to operational goals.
5. New employees are particularly susceptible to training. Older employees facing new job situations require specific training, as well as having need for development and growth opportunities.
6. Training needs require continuous monitoring.
7. The training officer of an agency is a professional with a responsibility to assist supervisors in solving training problems.

8. Many of the self-development steps important to the supervisor's own growth are equally important to the development of peers and subordinates. Knowledge of these is important when the supervisor consults with others on development and growth opportunities.

G. Health, Safety, and Accident Prevention

1. Management-minded supervisors take appropriate measures to assist employees in maintaining health and in assuring safe practices in the work environment.
2. Effective safety training and practices help to avoid injury and accidents.
3. Safety should be a management goal. All infractions of safety which are observed should be corrected without exception.
4. Employees' safety attitude, training and instruction, provision of safe tools and equipment, supervision, and leadership are considered highly important factors which contribute to safety and which can be influenced directly by supervisors.
5. When accidents do occur, they should be investigated promptly for very important reasons, including the fact that information which is gained can be used to prevent accidents in the future.

H. Equal Employment Opportunity

1. The supervisor should endeavor to treat all employees fairly, without regard to religion, race, sex, or national origin.
2. Groups tend to reflect the attitude of the leader. Prejudice can be detected even in very subtle form. Supervisors must strive to create a feeling of mutual respect and confidence in every employee.
3. Complete utilization of all human resources is a national goal. Equitable consideration should be accorded women in the work force, minority-group members, the physically and mentally handicapped, and the older employee. The important question is: "Who can do the job?"
4. Training opportunities, recognition for performance, overtime assignments, promotional opportunities, and all other personnel actions are to be handled on an equitable basis.

I. Improving Communications

1. Communications is achieving understanding between the sender and the receiver of a message. It also means sharing information—the creation of understanding.
2. Communication is basic to all human activity. Words are means of conveying meanings; however, real meanings are in people.
3. There are very practical differences in the effectiveness of one-way, impersonal, and two-way communications. Words spoken face-to-face are better understood. Telephone conversations are effective, but lack the rapport of person-to-person exchanges. The whole person communicates.
4. Cooperation and communication in an organization go hand in hand. When there is a mutual respect between people, spelling out rules and procedures for communicating is unnecessary.
5. There are several barriers to effective communications. These include failure to listen with respect and understanding, lack of skill in feedback, and misinterpreting the meanings of words used by the speaker. It is also common

practice to listen to what we want to hear, and tune out things we do not want to hear.

6. Communication is management's chief problem. The supervisor should accept the challenge to communicate more effectively and to improve interagency and intra-agency communications.
7. The supervisor may often plan for and conduct meetings. The planning phase is critical and may determine the success or the failure of a meeting.
8. Speaking before groups usually requires extra effort. Stage fright may never disappear completely, but it can be controlled.

J. Self-Development

1. Every employee is responsible for his own self-development.
2. Toastmaster and toastmistress clubs offer opportunities to improve skills in oral communications.
3. Planning for one's own self-development is of vital importance. Supervisors know their own strengths and limitations better than anyone else.
4. Many opportunities are open to aid the supervisor in his developmental efforts, including job assignments; training opportunities, both governmental and non-governmental—to include universities and professional conferences and seminars.
5. Programmed instruction offers a means of studying at one's own rate.
6. Where difficulties may arise from a supervisor's being away from his work for training, he may participate in televised home study or correspondence courses to meet his self-development needs.

K. Teaching and Training

1. The Teaching Process

Teaching is encouraging and guiding the learning activities of students toward established goals. In most cases this process consists of five steps: preparation, presentation, summarization, evaluation, and application.

a. Preparation

Preparation is two-fold in nature; that of the supervisor and the employee. Preparation by the supervisor is absolutely essential to success. He must know what, when, where, how, and whom he will teach. Some of the factors that should be considered are:

1) The objectives
2) The materials needed
3) The methods to be used
4) Employee participation
5) Employee interest
6) Training aids
7) Evaluation
8) Summarization

Employee preparation consists in preparing the employee to receive the material. Probably the most important single factor in the preparation of the employee is arousing and maintaining his interest. He must know the objectives of the training, why he is there, how the material can be used, and its importance to him.

b. Presentation
In presentation, have a carefully designed plan and follow it. The plan should be accurate and complete, yet flexible enough to meet situations as they arise. The method of presentation will be determined by the particular situation and objectives.

c. Summary
A summary should be made at the end of every training unit and program. In addition, there may be internal summaries depending on the nature of the material being taught. The important thing is that the trainee must always be able to understand how each part of the new material relates to the whole.

d. Application
The supervisor must arrange work so the employee will be given a chance to apply new knowledge or skills while the material is still clear in his mind and interest is high. The trainee does not really know whether he has learned the material until he has been given a chance to apply it. If the material is not applied, it loses most of its value.

e. Evaluation
The purpose of all training is to promote learning. To determine whether the training has been a success or failure, the supervisor must evaluate this learning.
In the broadest sense, evaluation includes all the devices, methods, skills, and techniques used by the supervisor to keep himself and the employees informed as to their progress toward the objectives they are pursuing. The extent to which the employee has mastered the knowledge, skills, and abilities, or changed his attitudes, as determined by the program objectives, is the extent to which instruction has succeeded or failed.
Evaluation should not be confined to the end of the lesson, day, or program but should be used continuously. We shall note later the way this relates to the rest of the teaching process.

2. Teaching Methods
A teaching method is a pattern of identifiable student and instructor activity used in presenting training material.
All supervisors are faced with the problem of deciding which method should be used at a given time.

a. Lecture
The lecture is direct oral presentation of material by the supervisor. The present trend is to place less emphasis on the trainer's activity and more on that of the trainee.

b. Discussion
Teaching by discussion or conference involves using questions and other techniques to arouse interest and focus attention upon certain areas, and by doing so creating a learning situation. This can be one of the most

valuable methods because it gives the employees an opportunity to express their ideas and pool their knowledge.

c. Demonstration
The demonstration is used to teach how something works or how to do something. It can be used to show a principle or what the results of a series of actions will be. A well-staged demonstration is particularly effective because it shows proper methods of performance in a realistic manner.

d. Performance
Performance is one of the most fundamental of all learning techniques or teaching methods. The trainee may be able to tell how a specific operation should be performed but he cannot be sure he knows how to perform the operation until he has done so.
As with all methods, there are certain advantages and disadvantages to each method.

e. Which Method to Use
Moreover, there are other methods and techniques of teaching. It is difficult to use any method without other methods entering into it. In any learning situation, a combination of methods is usually more effective than any one method alone.

Finally, evaluation must be integrated into the other aspects of the teaching-learning process.

It must be used in the motivation of the trainees; it must be used to assist in developing understanding during the training; and it must be related to employee application of the results of training.

This is distinctly the role of the supervisor.

www.ingramcontent.com/pod-product-compliance
Lightning Source LLC
Chambersburg PA
CBHW082041300426
44117CB00015B/2565